Understanding the Bible

UNDERSTANDING THE BIBLE

A Catholic Guide to
Applying God's Word
to Your Life Today

FR. JEFFREY KIRBY, STD

Our Sunday Visitor
Huntington, Indiana

Nihil Obstat
Msgr. Michael Heintz, Ph.D.
Censor Librorum

Imprimatur
✠ Kevin C. Rhoades
Bishop of Fort Wayne-South Bend
January 19, 2022

The *Nihil Obstat* and *Imprimatur* are official declarations that a book is free from doctrinal or moral error. It is not implied that those who have granted the *Nihil Obstat* and *Imprimatur* agree with the contents, opinions, or statements expressed.

Except where noted, the Scripture citations used in this work are taken from the *Revised Standard Version of the Bible — Second Catholic Edition* (Ignatius Edition), copyright © 1965, 1966, 2006 National Council of the Churches of Christ in the United States of America. Used by permission. All rights reserved.

Our Sunday Visitor Publishing Division, Our Sunday Visitor, Inc., 200 Noll Plaza, Huntington, IN 46750; www.osv.com; 1-800-348-2440

ISBN: 978-1-68192-980-4 (Inventory No. T2717)
1. RELIGION—Biblical Reference—General.
2. RELIGION—Biblical Studies—Bible Study Guides.
3. RELIGION—Christianity—Catholic.
eISBN: 978-1-68192-981-1
LCCN: 2021953352

Cover design: Tyler Ottinger
Interior design: Amanda Falk
Cover and interior art: AdobeStock

PRINTED IN THE UNITED STATES OF AMERICA

To the Kubic Family:

Ryan, Linni, Gabriel, Mary, and Philomena

Contents

Introduction   11

OLD TESTAMENT:
The Preparation for the Anointed Savior

The Pentateuch
     Genesis   22
     Exodus   27
     Leviticus   31
     Numbers   35
     Deuteronomy   39

Historical Books
     Joshua   44
     Judges   48
     Ruth   53
     First Samuel   57
     Second Samuel   61
     First Kings   65
     Second Kings   69
     First Chronicles   73
     Second Chronicles   77
     Ezra   81
     Nehemiah   85
     Tobit   89
     Judith   93
     Esther   97
     First Maccabees   101
     Second Maccabees   105

Wisdom Books
     Job   110
     Psalms   114

Proverbs   118
Ecclesiastes   122
Song of Solomon   126
Wisdom   129
Sirach   133

Prophetic Books
Isaiah   138
Jeremiah   142
Lamentations   146
Baruch   150
Ezekiel   154
Daniel   158
Hosea   162
Joel   166
Amos   170
Obadiah   174
Jonah   178
Micah   182
Nahum   186
Habakkuk   190
Zephaniah   194
Haggai   198
Zechariah   202
Malachi   206

NEW TESTAMENT:
The Life and Teachings of the Anointed Savior
and the Witness of the Early Church

The Gospels
Gospel of Matthew   214
Gospel of Mark   218
Gospel of Luke   222
Gospel of John   226

Historical Book

    Acts of the Apostles   232

Letters of Saint Paul

    Romans   238
    First Corinthians   242
    Second Corinthians   246
    Galatians   250
    Ephesians   254
    Philippians   258
    Colossians   261
    First Thessalonians   265
    Second Thessalonians   269
    First Timothy   272
    Second Timothy   276
    Titus   280
    Philemon   283
    Hebrews   287

Universal Letters

    James   292
    First Peter   295
    Second Peter   299
    First John   303
    Second John   306
    Third John   310
    Jude   313

Apocalyptic Book

    Revelation   318

Conclusion   322
Appendix A   327
Appendix B   329
Bibliography   331

Introduction

All Scripture is inspired by God and profitable for teaching, for reproof, for correction, and for training in righteousness, that the man of God may be complete, equipped for every good work.

2 TIMOTHY 3:16–17

Thank you for opening this book and for your interest in the Bible! This work is a heartfelt effort of a fellow believer in Jesus Christ — and a priestly shepherd of the Christian Faith — to make the Bible as accessible, understandable, livable, and enjoyable as possible. There is no high theology or specialized interpretation in its pages. It is a simple book with an ordinary — but powerful — mission: to help the People of God to know the Bible without intimidation or confusion. More specifically, its mission is to help you to know the Bible and be able to receive its wisdom and guidance in your life today.

Perhaps you've already tried reading the Bible and have been overwhelmed. Maybe you've read children's versions of it and want to go deeper, but you don't know how. Possibly you've been moved in your heart to pick up the Bible, knowing its eternal value, but have felt it to be beyond comprehension or navigation. Maybe you've read some of the Bible but don't understand how its wisdom is to be lived or applied in our world (or your life) today.

If any of these are the case, or something similar, then you're in good company!

"Do You Understand What You Are Reading?"

In the Acts of the Apostles, we're told about a powerful Ethiopian eunuch (8:26–39). He was in charge of the queen's treasury and had come to Jerusalem for worship. While returning home, he was sitting in his chariot, trying to read the prophet Isaiah. The Lord sent the apostle Philip to him and, when Philip heard the eunuch's attempt to read the Scriptures, he asked him, "Do you understand what you are reading?" In response, the court official said, "How can I, unless some one guides me?" (Acts 8:30–31).

The eunuch didn't understand what he was reading, but he was open to receiving help. Through the teaching of the apostle, the Scriptures came alive to the eunuch and made sense to him. The experience was so profound that he asked for baptism on the spot!

In a similar way, you've likely waded through some difficulties and confusion in trying to comprehend the Sacred Scriptures. So I hope this book can provide you with some guidance in understanding the Bible, the story of salvation contained in its narrative, its eternal wisdom, and its application to our lives today.

"All Scripture Is Inspired ..."

The Bible is the written word of God. It contains the account of how God has revealed himself to humanity through his words and deeds throughout salvation history. The Bible shows us the depths of God's love and unveils to us his infinite goodness and beauty. It contains his constant invitation for us to be with him, to follow his ways, and to be members of his family.

The Bible has been called God's love letter to humanity. It is a living message that speaks words of love and truth to every heart. Its message goes out and does not come back empty (Is 55:11).

Saint Paul teaches us that the Bible "was written for our instruction, that by steadfastness and by the encouragement of the Scriptures we might have hope" (Rom 15:4).

Through the Bible, God continues to instruct us. He accompanies and teaches us. He guides us and helps us to persevere in hope. As Saint Paul also teaches, "all Scripture is inspired." This means that every word of the Bible is the breath of God. Although written in the language of man, it is the true and inerrant word of God. The Bible bears a true and trustworthy testimony of God, and so we can have confidence in it.

In light of such a blessed gift, this book will dissect the interior structure of the Bible. It will flesh out the revelation and wisdom contained within the sacred narrative and indicate how it can help us answer the questions or deal with the struggles in our own lives today.

"The Word Became Flesh ..."

As we study the Bible and dive into the splendor of its wisdom, we must always keep before us the powerful reality that this "Word became flesh" (Jn 1:14). Every truth that the Bible teaches is fulfilled and made flesh for us in Jesus Christ, the Eternal Word who became a man and lived among us. The truth contained in the Bible, therefore, is not abstract or removed from our lives.

The Lord Jesus lived among us! He loved with a human heart, worked with human hands, suffered in a human body, and cried human tears. Every truth in the Bible has a lived reality, and we can see that reality in the life of Jesus Christ, and his life is the definitive way in which we can understand and live out the truth of Sacred Scripture.

Outline of This Book

Now, about the structure of this book: Great effort was put into making it as approachable as possible. Because of this, each of the seventy-three short chapters explores the respective seventy-three books of the Bible.

Although the Bible is one shared message, it is also a library, with each of its books having its own literary genre, context, and message. As such, it's good to look at each book on its own merit, while not forgetting that each book is only one part of God's overall message to humanity.

As we learn about each book of the Bible, we can apply its divine message to our lives.

With this in mind, each chapter will provide:

- An Opening Prayer and Basic Message relating to the book of the Bible
- An Introductory Overview, which will provide the general point or purpose of the biblical book
- A Basic Outline of the respective book
- An Application to Our Lives, which will propose a way in which the biblical book's wisdom can help us in our lives today
- Some Basic Points and notes for Getting Started on the particular biblical book
- A Concluding Prayer

Before starting, it might be good to go over a few basic points about the Bible.

Some Bible Basics

Here are some fundamental points about the Bible. Although these are principally given for new Bible readers, they can provide a quick review for all of us:

- The Bible ("book") is called by many names, including "Sacred Scripture" (singular to designate its unity), "Sacred Scriptures" (plural to designate its diversity of books), "the Word," and "the Good Book."

- The Bible can be viewed as a type of library since it contains multiple books of different types and styles from different time periods and authors.
- It consists of two main parts: the Old Testament and the New Testament.
- The Old Testament prepared the way for the long-awaited Anointed Savior (the Messiah). The New Testament shows us Jesus as the Anointed Savior and tells us about his life and teachings.
- The Old Testament has forty-six books, and the New Testament has twenty-seven books.
- The Protestant tradition only has thirty-nine books in the Old Testament. This is different from the official list in the Catholic Bible. (See Appendix B for an explanation.)
- The books of the Bible are not structured to be read in chronological order.
- There are narrative books and supplemental books. All of the books are the inspired Word of God.
- The narrative books give the basic storyline of salvation history. (See Appendix A for the list of the narrative books.)
- The supplemental books develop a specific part or theme of salvation history.
- Each book of the Bible has its own literary structure, purpose, context, and theme.
- In a Bible citation, such as John 3:16, the book is given first (in this case, John), the chapter is second (3), and the verse or verses are third (16). Sometimes a lowercase letter *a* or *b* is given after

16

the verse. This means that only a portion of the verse is cited, indicating the beginning (a) or the end (b) of the verse.

- When you are looking for a specific chapter or verse in your Bible, remember that the chapters are usually large numbers (sometimes in bold) within the book. The verses are the small numbers within a chapter.

- If you're not sure where a biblical book is located, you can refer to the table of contents at the beginning of most Bibles. Sometimes a particular Bible will use abbreviations for books. These abbreviations are also provided at the beginning of most Bibles.

- Don't be surprised if you read different Bibles and find the wording different. There are many translations of the Bible. Different translations might have different source documents, or prefer certain wording over others, or have a specific emphasis. There are pros and cons for each translation. The New American Bible is the translation that's used in the Mass. Many people use the Revised Standard Version of the Bible — Second Catholic Edition (Ignatius Edition) for study and personal reading of the Bible. This is the translation we're using in this book. Over and above academic debates, however, the best translation of the Bible is the one you're reading!

- In addition, do not be confused if you come across different orderings of the books of the Old Testament. Some translations put 1 and 2 Maccabees at the end of the prophetic books. In this book, we have followed the order that places them within the historical books.

With these basics completed, let's start our reading and application of the Bible to our lives today! Our first book is Genesis, the very first book of the Bible. It's time — let's begin!

OLD TESTAMENT

The Preparation for
the Anointed Savior

The Pentateuch

Genesis*
Exodus
Leviticus
Numbers
Deuteronomy

---

*Genesis, Exodus, and Numbers are narrative books of the Bible.

Genesis

*And he journeyed on from the Negeb as far as Bethel, to
the place where his tent had been at the beginning, between
Bethel and Ai, to the place where he had made an altar at
the first; and there Abram called on the name of the LORD.*

GENESIS 13:3–4

Opening Prayer
God Most High,
you always call us to yourself.
You blessed the patriarchs of old
and revealed your plan of salvation.
Help us to rely on your will.
We trust in you.
Through Christ our Lord.
Amen.

Basic Message
God created us to be in his family. He wants to bless us, although
our sins frustrate his plan.

Introductory Overview
Genesis describes God's creation of the world and of the human family. Using figurative language, it recounts the rebellion
against God and humanity's sinfulness. Such sinfulness is depicted in Adam and Eve, in their initial posterity, as well as in the
patriarch Abraham and his descendants.

Basic Outline

The Book of Genesis consists of two main parts:

- Chapters 1–11 (commonly called "the early world"): The earliest accounts of creation, the Fall of humanity from God's grace, the Great Flood, the Tower of Babel, and other stories that show the battle between God's will and humanity's pride.
- Chapters 12–50 ("The patriarchs"): The narrative of God's call to Abraham (12–25), Isaac (25–26), Jacob (26–50), and the blessings or drama brought about by their obedience or disobedience to God's will.

Application to Our Lives

Genesis 12 is a turning point in the story of salvation. It marks the end of the early world and the beginning of the time of the patriarchs. The time period begins with Abraham and his call to leave his hometown of Ur — his people, language, food, comfort zone, and everything he knows — to go to a land that he does not know (12:1–9). Abraham obeys. When he arrives in the Promised Land, about a thousand miles from his home, he builds altars and wants God to be first in his life (12:7–8). Then a famine strikes the land (12:10). Rather than turning to God and using the altars he built, Abraham abandons the land to which God called him and flees to Egypt. After some hard lessons in Egypt, Abraham returns to the Promised Land, repents, and worships the living God (13:3–4).

In our lives, when we try to obey God, things will not always be easy. Sometimes we face our own "famines," such as heartbreaks, disappointments, financial struggles, difficult relationships, bad health, the list goes on. If we're not careful, we can regret doing the right thing. We can think that God has failed us. We can ignore him and "flee to Egypt." But God is with us. The strength and help that we need is always before us if we turn to him. Abraham, our father in faith, had to learn this hard lesson. Sometimes we do too, but God is waiting and always calling us to himself. Life will not be easy. This is a fallen world, but the grace we need to obey God and to persevere in doing good things is always available to us, if we ask for it. God waits for us. We need to turn to him.

Basic Points

Author: The Jewish and Christian traditions attribute the Book of Genesis to Moses, although several editors worked on the book through the ages.

Placement: Genesis is the first book of the Old Testament. It is part of what is called "the Torah" or "the Pentateuch" — names given to the first five books of the Old Testament. Genesis is also the first narrative book of the Bible. (See Appendix A.)

Keywords:

- Figurative language: A literary genre in which a symbol, sign, or image is used to represent a truth or lesson. It is often used in sacred literature to point to a truth that is beyond human language or popular speech.
- Anointed Savior: After the Fall of our first parents, God gave humanity the promise of an Anointed Savior (called *Messiah* in Hebrew and *Christ* in Greek). The Savior would heal humanity from its sins, although he would suffer (see 3:15). The whole course of salvation history is the gradual preparation by God for the human family to receive this Anointed Savior.

- Patriarch: The eldest male member of an extended family, who is revered for his wisdom. In the ancient world, patriarchs were often chiefs of their own tribe. Abraham was the first patriarch in a series of patriarchs in early salvation history.
- Abraham's promises: God extended the promise of an Anointed Savior to Abraham. He also promised him land, a royal dynasty, and a universal blessing. These promises develop within the course of salvation history and are ultimately fulfilled in Jesus Christ.
- Judah: The fourth son of Jacob (29:35). God gives his special blessing to Abraham, who, in turn, gives it to his son Isaac, and then Isaac to his son Jacob, whom God renames Israel (32:28). Jacob then confers the universal blessing on Judah and his descendants (49:8–10). These promises and prophecies are all later fulfilled in Jesus Christ, son of Abraham and son of Judah (see Mt 1:1–2; Jn 3:16–17).

Getting Started

While the eventual goal is to read all fifty chapters of Genesis, here are three selections that can get us started. Each selection shows us the depth and wisdom of Genesis: the creation and Fall of humanity (chapters 2–3); the test of Abraham (chapter 22); and the mercy of Joseph and his reconciliation with his brothers (chapters 42–45).

Concluding Prayer

Eternal Father,
God of Abraham, Isaac, and Jacob,
come to us,
teach us to trust you,
especially when things are difficult or confusing.

Help us to turn to you in our hardships,
to rely on you in our difficulties,
and to depend on your grace in our anxieties.
You are the Father of all.
We love you. We praise you. We thank you.
Through Christ our Lord.
Amen.

Exodus

And now, behold, the cry of the sons of Israel has come to me, and I have seen the oppression with which the Egyptians oppress them. Come, I will send you to Pharaoh that you may bring forth my people, the sons of Israel, out of Egypt.

EXODUS 3:9–10

Opening Prayer
Eternal Father,
you seek out what is lost.
When your people were enslaved,
you heard their plea,
and came to their rescue.
Help us to turn to you in our darkness.
Come to us. Save us.
Through Christ our Lord.
Amen.

Basic Message
God hears our cries and seeks to save us in our distress. He wants to ransom us, but we have to trust and obey him.

Introductory Overview
Exodus describes the four hundred years of slavery that God's people endured in Egypt and God's saving action as he liberates them and teaches them how to live as his children.

Basic Outline

The Book of Exodus consists of two main parts:

- Chapters 1–18: The enslavement of God's people for four hundred years, the raising up of Moses as a leader, and the ten plagues against Pharaoh and the gods of Egypt. This section concludes with the Passover, when God spared from death the firstborn sons of Israel and freed his Chosen People from slavery and lead them through the Red Sea to begin their quest for the Promised Land.
- Chapters 19–40: The covenant at Mount Sinai, the giving of the Ten Commandments, and the building of the tabernacle (a series of tents that surrounded the place of worship) and the Ark of the Covenant (a golden box-shaped vessel that held the presence of God on earth).

Application to Our Lives

In Exodus 3, God calls Moses to a special mission (3:9–10). Moses was a Hebrew who had been raised as an Egyptian nobleman. He fled Egypt after committing a murder. He lost everything he knew. Moses was living in a desert wilderness and working for his father-in-law as a shepherd. We can say that he was down and out. It was precisely in this context — far from perfect — that God came to him.

Moses wasn't looking for the God of his forefathers, but God was looking for him. He wasn't pursuing a new profession or laboring to find something different in his life, but God had a plan for him. The Lord God called to Moses, revealed himself to him, and sent him on one of the most important missions in salvation history. Moses was hesitant. He didn't know what to say, and he had a speech impediment, but God trusted in him and asked him to go. Moses relented and eventually led his people out of slavery and back to the Promised Land of their forefathers. In our lives, we can experience a lot of brokenness and displacement. We can be down and out. And yet God knows where we are; he loves us, comes to each of us, and has a mission for us. We may not readily want to accept his call, but he sees more in us than we can see in ourselves. God has confidence in us, and he will continue to call us to himself and to the mission he has for us.

Basic Points

Author: The Jewish and Christian traditions attribute the Book of Exodus to Moses, although several editors worked on the book through the ages.

Placement: Exodus is the second book of the Old Testament. It is part of what is called "the Torah" or "the Pentateuch," which are the names given to the first five books of the Old Testament. Exodus is also the second narrative book of the Bible. (See Appendix A.)

Keywords:

- Covenant: A solemn agreement between two parties in which each party becomes a member of the other party's family.
- Passover: The annual liturgical "reenactment" of God's saving his people from slavery in Egypt and his ransoming the firstborn sons of his people. It would later be fulfilled in the passion, death, and resurrection of Jesus Christ.

Getting Started

While the eventual goal is to read all forty chapters of Exodus, here are three selections that can get us started. Each selection shows us the depth and wisdom of Exodus: God calls Moses and reveals his Holy Name (chapter 3); the "Song of the Sea," the first song of praise in the Bible (15:1–21); and God communicating with Moses in the tent of meeting "as one speaks to a friend" (33:7–11).

Concluding Prayer

Everlasting Father,
you are the great I AM!
You call to us.
You seek to ransom us.
You desire us to be in your family.
You invite us to speak with you as a friend.
Help us to turn to you. Help us to trust you.
Through Christ our Lord.
Amen.

Leviticus

You are to distinguish between the holy and the common, and between the unclean and the clean; and you are to teach the sons of Israel all the statutes which the LORD has spoken to them by Moses.

LEVITICUS 10:10–11

Opening Prayer

All-holy God,
you love us and call us to yourself.
You desire to make us holy,
as you are holy.
Show us your face!
Have mercy on us.
Give us the help of your grace.
Through Christ our Lord.
Amen.

Basic Message

God is holy, and we must approach him as he directs us, since we cannot approach him on our own merit.

Introductory Overview

Leviticus is basically the ritual book for the Levites, the tribe of Israel that was entrusted with the priesthood after the tribe refused to worship the golden calf at Mount Sinai (Ex 32). Leviticus describes the rituals, priesthood, and purity laws that must be followed if a person desires to encounter and worship God.

Basic Outline

As a ritual book for priests, Leviticus is structurally written. There are three inverse parts, emphasizing the sacrificial worship that was central to the life of the Israelites, and a conclusion that calls God's people to be faithful. The three inverse parts are designed to accentuate Yom Kippur, or the Day of Atonement (16), the annual feast that commemorates the forgiveness of the people's sins, including those of the high priest, and the restoration of their Old Covenant holiness.

- Chapters 1–7 and 23–25: The ritual sacrifices and feast days of Israel.
- Chapters 8–10 and 21–22: The ordination and qualifications of priests.
- Chapters 11–12 and 17–20: The ritual and moral purity that is expected of the Israelites as they worship and serve God.
- Chapters 26–27: A call to serve God faithfully and so keep his covenant.

Application to Our Lives

Only Aaron and his sons, and their direct male descendants in the tribe of Levi, could serve as priests in the wilderness tabernacle (Ex 28:1–4, 40–43). In Leviticus 10, we read about Nadab and Abihu, Aaron's sons who offend God in offering incense, which likely included their being drunk (1–11).

In response to their wrongdoing, God strikes the two priests dead (Lv 10:2). In addition, Moses forbids Aaron and his two other sons, Eleazar and Ithamar, from publicly mourning Nadab and Abihu, although he permits the other Israelites to do so (10:6–7). Although such disciplines are severe, God shows his people how important holiness is in offering true worship.

God speaks to Aaron — and not to Moses, as he normally does — and explains that Israel must know the difference between the things of God and those of this world (10:8–11). Such teaching is especially important for the priests of Israel, all of whom have been chosen and blessed by God.

In our lives, we must be prudent when consuming alcohol and other things that might cloud our judgment and lead us to say or do things that we later regret. The abuse of alcohol likely caused the sons of Aaron to be distracted in fulfilling their duties reverently. We must judiciously use the things of this world and so fulfill our duties with strong virtue. We must also realize how seriously God takes worship, and how we should conduct ourselves during sacred liturgies. We have to keep before us the distinction between the things of God and the things of this world, between holy things and sinful things, and then faithfully follow the path of God.

Basic Points

Author: The Jewish and Christian traditions attribute the Book of Leviticus to Moses, although several editors worked on the book through the ages.

Placement: Leviticus is the third book of the Old Testament. It is part of what is called "the Torah" or "the Pentateuch," names given to the first five books of the Old Testament. Leviticus is a supplemental book of the principal narrative books of the Bible.

Keywords:

- Holiness: The way of life by which a child of God is separated from sin and evil so as to be in God's presence and have fellowship with him.

- Day of Atonement: One of the highest feast days of ancient Israel. On the holy day, a goat would be offered in reparation for the sins of God's people. Its blood would be sprinkled on the Ark of the Covenant, which contained God's presence on earth. A second goat — the scapegoat — would have the sins of Israel spoken over it, and then it would be released into the desert wilderness. The Day of Atonement is the central part of the Book of Leviticus.

Getting Started

While the eventual goal is to read all twenty-seven chapters Leviticus, here are three selections that can get us started. Each selection shows us the depth and wisdom of Leviticus: the "thanksgiving sacrifice," which was offered in remembrance of God's blessings and represented one of the sacrifices that non-priests could eat (7:12–15); the moral life that God was calling forth from his children (chapters 18–20); and Moses' exhortation to fidelity (chapters 26–27).

Concluding Prayer

Ever-living God,
you are all-holy!
You seek to make us holy.
Help us to turn to you.
Grant us the grace to pursue you.
Guide us along your way.
Show us your glory!
Through Christ our Lord.
Amen.

Numbers

*And the L*ORD *said to Moses and Aaron, "Because you did not believe in me, to sanctify me in the eyes of the sons of Israel, therefore you shall not bring this assembly into the land which I have given them."*

NUMBERS 20:12

Opening Prayer
Heavenly Father,
you always journey with your people.
You never abandon us.
You walk with us and guide us.
Help us to recognize your presence,
to accept your grace,
and to stay faithful to you throughout our lives.
Through Christ our Lord.
Amen.

Basic Message
God is patient and loving. He will mold and shape his people, sometimes through discipline, so that they can share in his holiness.

Introductory Overview
Numbers includes the historical account of the forty years that God's people spent in the desert as they were being purified of their idolatry and faithlessness and so prepared to enter the

Promised Land of their forefathers Abraham, Isaac, and Jacob.

Basic Outline
As a book that includes the forty-year journey of God's people through the desert, the Book of Numbers is a fluid narrative. As such, there are five internal parts within the book. Three consist of locations, and two are intervals that summarize events while the people traveled to a new location.

- Chapters 1–10: God's people at Mount Sinai, census of God's people, arrangement for the camp, and development of purity laws from Leviticus.
- Chapters 10–12: God's people travel as the Divine Presence guides them. The journey is marked by multiple complaints of the people, who argue that things were better in Egypt.
- Chapters 13–19: God's people dwell in the wilderness of Paran.
- Chapters 20–21: God's people travel again. The journey is again marked by complaints and rebellion.
- Chapters 22–36: God's people on the plains of Moab.

Application to Our Lives
In Numbers 20, God's people complain that there is no water. They threaten rebellion against Moses. In response, God tells Moses to go before the people and talk to a rock (20:8). Yes, the request is peculiar, and Moses thinks so too. God wants Moses to speak to the rock so that he can provide water for his people. He wants it to be clear that the water is not coming from any natural source. It will be a clear sign of God's holiness and of his love and care for his people.

Moses, however, refuses to trust in God. Rather than talking to the rock, he strikes it twice with his staff. Water flows from the

rock (20:11), and the people drink freely. Thus, Moses puts the people's focus on himself, rather than on God.

Because he did not trust and obey the Lord, Moses could not enter the Promised Land. Rather, like the rest of those in his generation, he died in the desert.

In our lives, we are called to listen to the Lord and trust in him. We have to follow what he commands, so that we can see his holiness and goodness in our lives. We have to be cautious in thinking that worldly success, human praise, or respectability are the conditions of goodness. Oftentimes, we can disobey God, cause harm to others, and still have "success" in this world. The people thought Moses was great, but his supposed greatness came at a great cost, and it was not worth it. We have to show the boldness of the children of God and confidently rely on the teachings and guidance of God, no matter how peculiar or uncomfortable it may seem.

Basic Points

Author: The Jewish and Christian traditions attribute the Book of Numbers to Moses, although several editors worked on the book through the ages.

Placement: Numbers is the fourth book of the Old Testament. It is part of what is called "the Torah" or "the Pentateuch," which are the names given to the first five books of the Old Testament. Numbers is the third narrative book of the Bible. (See Appendix A.)

Keywords:

- Rebellion: The spiritual act by which a person refuses to show trust in and obedience to the ways of God. It includes a false belief that someone, something, or some worldly benefit is higher than the love we owe God.

- Promised Land: The land formally entrusted by God to Abraham. It was one of three blessings that God gave to the first patriarch. It is the homeland of God's people.

Getting Started

While the eventual goal is to read all thirty-six chapters of Numbers, here are two selections that can get us started. Each selection shows us the depth and wisdom of Numbers: the presence of God under the appearance of cloud and fire, through which God lived with his people and literally guided them through the desert (9:15–23), and the failed attempt of Balaam, a pagan seer, to denounce God's people. Every time he tried, he ended up only blessing God's people (chapters 22–24).

Concluding Prayer

God of the wilderness and the desert,
you are always with your people.
You journey with us.
You choose to accompany us.
You care for us. You love us.
You manifest your goodness and holiness
to us in countless ways.
We seek to follow you!
Help us to trust you. Strengthen us.
Through Christ our Lord.
Amen.

Deuteronomy

*Hear, O Israel: The L*ORD *our God is one L*ORD*; and you shall love the L*ORD *your God with all your heart, and with all your soul, and with all your might.*

DEUTERONOMY 6:4–5

Opening Prayer
Eternal Father,
you who are wisdom and power itself,
guide our weak and wavering hearts.
Enlighten us.
Help us to know how to live as your children.
Show us your path of light and truth.
Instruct us. Teach us.
Give us the strength to love you alone.
Through Christ our Lord.
Amen.

Basic Message
There is only one God, who must be loved above all things. In spite of the many things that want our complete hearts, our hearts belong only to God.

Introductory Overview
Deuteronomy is the last will and testament of a dying Moses. He is speaking to the new generation of God's people, who were born during the purification in the desert and who will very

shortly enter the Promised Land. Moses is teaching them how to live as the children of God by recalling the deeds and laws of God over the past forty years.

Basic Outline

The Book of Deuteronomy consists of three principal speeches given by Moses:

- Chapters 1–11: Moses' opening speech to the children of the desert, recalling the deeds and teachings of God as they prepare to enter the Promised Land.
- Chapters 12–26: Review of the various laws of the covenant and a reminder to the new generation of how they are to live as the children of God.
- Chapters 27–34: Conclusion of Moses' teachings, a warning to the people to be faithful to God; prophecy about the future; and the death of Moses.

Application to Our Lives

In Deuteronomy 6, Moses gives the highest summary of the teachings and laws of God in what is called the *Shema* (6:4–5). The Shema is a declaration that God is one and that he alone is to be loved and worshiped above all things with our whole being. Moses gives the Shema as a reminder of how we are to approach God. In the historical context, Moses gives the Shema to preserve God's people from idolatry as they were about to enter the Promised Land, which was occupied by cultures with many pagan gods and goddesses.

The Shema is so revered that it is both a moral teaching and a prayer at the same time. It is a guide for how to live as well as a prayer that includes all the aspirations of our hearts.

The Shema has always been a challenge for fallen humanity. In our lives, we need to hear the invitation that God is giving us.

He asks us to give him our whole being. As God is all-good and all-holy, he will take what is offered bless it, heal it, restore it, and make it better and holier. Nothing else can do this for us. The things of this world and the false gods of any age promise us everything but ultimately give nothing but misery and heartache. God does not want us to suffer in this way. And so he calls us to himself. He asks us to trust him and surrender to his goodness. The Shema is a moral teaching and prayer for us today. We are challenged by it, but we are called to accept it and then do our best to love God above all things with our whole being.

Basic Points

Author: The Jewish and Christian traditions attribute the Book of Deuteronomy to Moses (and the conclusion to Joshua, after Moses dies), although several editors worked on the book through the ages.

Placement: Deuteronomy is the fifth book of the Old Testament. It is the conclusion of what is called "the Torah" or "the Pentateuch," which are the names given to the first five books of the Old Testament. Deuteronomy is a supplemental book of the Bible.

Keywords:

- Second Law: The translated name of *Deuteronomy*. It is called a second law since Moses was summarizing and applying the laws of God's covenant to a new generation.
- Canaan: A name given to the Promised Land. Its inhabitants, the Canaanites, were known for their multiple false gods, whose stories were used to justify sexual perversity, child sacrifice, and other evils.

Getting Started

While the eventual goal is to read all thirty-four chapters of the Book of Deuteronomy, here are three selections that can get us started. Each selection shows us the depth and wisdom of Deuteronomy: the warning of Moses not to forget God in times of prosperity (chapter 8); the teaching on tithes, with an emphasis on the poor — a unique focus of God's people, not found among other ancient religions (14:22–29); and Moses' call to accept the abundant life offered by God (30:11–20).

Concluding Prayer

Most loving, ever-living God,
you bless us with your goodness.
You teach us your truth.
You show us your love.
We surrender to you.
We give you all that we are.
We ask your blessing.
Come to us.
Show us your glory!
Through Christ our Lord.
Amen.

Historical Books

Joshua[*]
Judges
Ruth
First and Second Samuel
First and Second Kings
First and Second Chronicles
Ezra
Nehemiah
Tobit[†]
Judith
Esther
First Maccabees
Second Maccabees

---

[*]Joshua, Judges, First and Second Samuel, First and Second Kings, Ezra, Nehemiah, and First Maccabees are narrative books of the Bible. (See Appendix A.)
[†]Tobit, Judith, and First and Second Maccabees are deuterocanonical books. (See Appendix B.)

Joshua

Joshua went to him and said to him, "Are you for us, or for our adversaries?" And he said, "No; but as commander of the army of the LORD I have now come."

JOSHUA 5:13B–14A

Opening Prayer

All-powerful God,
you are a mighty warrior,
and the Prince of Peace.
You call for justice and goodness;
you command peace.
Help us to follow you faithfully.
May we always remember your kindness.
May we seek your mercy.
Show us your face.
Through Christ our Lord.
Amen.

Basic Message

God is faithful to his promises and is a warrior against evil and wickedness. In short, God seeks to dwell with his people and lead them to holiness.

Introductory Overview

The Book of Joshua tells how Joshua, the leader of God's people after Moses, shepherds the children of God into the Promised Land of their forefathers. It recounts the battles between the people of God and the Canaanites, which represent God's battle against evil. The book concludes with God's people occupying the Promised Land and Joshua dividing it up among the various tribes.

Basic Outline

The Book of Joshua consists of four main parts:

- Chapters 1–5: Joshua becomes the leader of the people of God. God's people miraculously cross the Jordan River and enter into the Promised Land.
- Chapters 6–12: God's people and the Canaanites battle each other. In particular, God teaches his people through the fall of Jericho and the battle at Ai.
- Chapters 13–22: Joshua divides up the Promised Land among the tribes of Israel.
- Chapters 23–24: Joshua makes his final address to the People of God, calling them to remain faithful to God's covenant. Joshua dies.

Application to Our Lives

In Joshua 5, God's people are preparing for battle with Jericho. God has already miraculously divided the Jordan River so that his people could enter into the Promised Land. On that occasion, God's people were able to celebrate Passover for the first time in the land of their forefathers. The people were consecrated to God again. It was a joyful occasion. Joshua was grateful, but he was also readying things for Jericho. It was uncertain how the mighty walls of the great city would fall.

On this occasion, Joshua comes across a man with his sword drawn. Joshua asks him which side he is on, that of the Israelites or that of the Canaanites (5:13b). The man responds, "No," and then goes on to explain that he is the commander of the army of the Lord of hosts (5:14). He is an angel, and he is teaching Joshua that God is not on any one human side. God is always on the side of righteousness and goodness. The Israelites' battles are not primarily against the Canaanites (nor are our battles against other human enemies today). They are against evil.

In our lives, we have to be careful about making things overly partisan. Every side has its aspects of truth, and every side has its areas of error. God rejects the proud, even if they're right. Yes, we can be right in our views but completely wrong in our approach. God is not on any one side of anything. He is above merely human distinctions and is the Father of everyone. He calls us all to truth and holiness. And so, as we disagree with others, or find ourselves in a different camp from our neighbor, it's worth reminding ourselves of the angelic warning. God is on no side. He seeks righteousness among all his children.

Basic Points

Author: The Jewish and Christian traditions attribute the Book of Joshua to Joshua, although several editors worked on the book through the ages.

Placement: Joshua is the sixth book of the Old Testament. It is part of what are called the historical books of the Bible. Joshua is the fourth of the principal narrative books of the Bible. (See Appendix A.)

Keywords:

- Israel: The name taken by God's people in honor of the great patriarch Jacob, who was renamed Israel by God (see Gn 32:28). Later, this title would be given to the Church (see Gal 6:15–16).
- Use of violence: In various parts of the Bible, there

is a call to violence for noble purposes. Such occasions were responses to grave evils, were tempered compared with the normal practices among ancient cultures, and were considered provisional and temporary. God was teaching his people within a state of affairs that they would understand. Such violence was never to be the norm. As God's moral law was intended to form his people through the ages, so they would begin to realize other ways to fight against evil. With this historical understanding in view, the Bible does not provide justification for religious violence.

Getting Started

While the eventual goal is to read all twenty-four chapters of Joshua, here are three selections that can get us started. Each selection shows us the depth and wisdom of Joshua: the comparison between the fall of Jericho, where God's people trusted in God, and the defeat of God's people at Ai, where they trusted only in themselves (chapters 6–7); the miracle of the sun (10:1–15); and Joshua's call for God's people to remain faithful (chapters 23–24).

Concluding Prayer

Father of all,
you fulfill your promises.
You come to our aid.
You are ever faithful and glorious in all you do.
Help us to know your truth.
Guide us to fight evil with virtue.
Strengthen us by your grace.
Show us your glory!
Through Christ our Lord.
Amen.

Judges

When Israel grew strong, they put the Canaanites to forced labor, but did not utterly drive them out.

JUDGES 1:28

Opening Prayer

Heavenly Father,
without you nothing has merit,
nothing is good.
Without you, we forget who we are.
You give us our dignity.
You show us how to live righteously.
You show us the way to peace.
Give us your grace.
Help us to follow you in all we do.
Show us your glory.
Through Christ our Lord.
Amen.

Basic Message

Disobedience and infidelity to the ways of God will lead people to behave in vile and wicked ways. In spite of humanity's wickedness, God is all-good and ever-faithful. He continues to work among his people.

Introductory Overview

The Book of Judges describes the regression first of the leadership and then of the whole people of God, as they abandon the ways of God and embrace the evils of the Canaanites. The book is tragic, violent, and not for the faint of heart. It concludes with a prophecy about kingship and hope for the future.

Basic Outline

The Book of Judges consists of three main parts:

- Chapters 1–2: The failure of God's people to remove all the tribes of the Canaanites and their influences and the death of Joshua.
- Chapters 3–16: The gradual moral and spiritual regression of Israel's leadership into the evil practices of the Canaanites.
- Chapters 17–21: Following the example of their leadership, God's people become corrupt and begin to live according to the ways of the Canaanites. The first civil war among God's people erupts.

Application to Our Lives

In Judges 1, the narrative describes the disobedience of God's people and their willingness to allow grave sin in their hearts and in the outward practices of their community. The People of God are still under God's command to remove the Canaanites and their influences from the Promised Land. As a help to understand this passage of the Bible, we could replace the word *Canaanite* with *grave sin*. God is calling his people to rid themselves of sin and its sway and, instead, to seek holiness.

God's people, however, got very comfortable very fast. After some initial battles and victories, they slowed down and eventually just settled. The Canaanites were left in place. Some were put to hard labor, while others were left to coexist among God's people (see 1:28). This had devastating consequences.

God's people began to lose their way. They allowed themselves to fall into a severe moral and spiritual downward spiral. They began to accept things that should have been unimaginable for a people trained and disciplined in the moral truth of the living God. For example, the judge Jephthah sacrificed his daughter, thinking that God wanted such a sacrifice (11:29–40). Tragically, God's people became indistinguishable from the Canaanites.

In our lives, God calls us to rid ourselves of sin and seek holiness in him. As with the Canaanites, we have to remove and keep at bay all influences that might cause us to sin, to normalize sin, or to justify sin in our lives or our communities. We are the children of God. We are summoned to be a holy people. The "spiritual Canaanites" in our lives today could be gossip, slander, anger, impurity, pornography, abuse of alcohol or prescription drugs, jealousy, the list goes on. We must have a healthy self-suspicion, examine our consciences, and ask ourselves the hard questions about the influence or effects things might have upon our hearts and spiritual well-being. This is true for ourselves and for our families and communities. As God's children, we are called to avoid evil and seek to grow in grace and holiness every day.

Basic Points

Author: The Jewish and Christian traditions attribute the Book of Judges to the prophet Samuel, although several editors worked on the book through the ages.

Placement: Judges is the seventh book of the Old Testament. It is part of what are called the historical books of the Bible. Judges is the fifth of the principal narrative books of the Bible. (See Appendix A.)

Keywords:

- Judge: The biblical title for the leaders of God's people in the Promised Land before the establishment of the monarchy. The judges were not judicial officials, but rather political-military leaders. The positions were not national offices and were not hereditary. A judge would be raised up by God for a specific battle or purpose.
- Sin cycle: The cycle described in the Book of Judges that reflects the instability of God's people. The cycle begins with sin and oppression. God's people would then repent. They would be delivered from their oppression and given peace. But then they would take the peace for granted and fall back into sin, and the cycle would continue.
- Spirit of the Lord: God's Spirit would sometimes inspire the judges of God's people to serve him and defend his covenant. It should be noted, however, that what some of the judges did with God's power was not pleasing to him. Simply because something is narrated in the Bible does not mean it has God's approval. God would never command something outside of his own moral law.

Getting Started

While the eventual goal is to read all twenty-one chapters of Judges, here are three selections that can get us started. Each selection shows us the depth and wisdom of Judges: the faithful service of the judge Deborah, the first female leader of God's people (chapters 4–5); the judge Jephthah and his infamous child sacrifice (chapter 11); and the story of the judge Samson, who was seduced by a woman of Canaan and allowed his strength to be taken from him (chapters 13–16).

Concluding Prayer

O God,
you are merciful and just.
You are slow to anger and abounding in kindness.
Look upon us in our fallenness.
Help us to turn to you.
Give us your strength to follow your way.
Strengthen us in your truth.
Console us by your grace.
Show us your glory!
Through Christ our Lord.
Amen.

Ruth

*Entreat me not to leave you or to return from following you;
for where you go I will go; and where you lodge I will lodge;
your people shall be my people, and your God my God.*

RUTH 1:16

Opening Prayer

All-loving God,
you call us to yourself
and then send us out to love one another.
Give us your Spirit.
Strengthen us with your grace.
Help us to love as you love
and to be faithful as you are faithful.
Grant us your peace.
Show us your face.
Through Christ our Lord.
Amen.

Basic Message

God's loving care for his children is always at work, even in the
normal, everyday affairs of life. God blesses those who are virtuous and kind.

Introductory Overview

The Book of Ruth describes the strong stock from which the future King David would come. It tells of the life of Ruth, a widow,

and her amazing love and loyalty toward her mother-in-law. Such loyalty is rewarded as she finds a new husband and is blessed with a son. The book is tender, inspiring, and filled with hope. It is a much-needed message after the darkness of the Book of Judges.

Basic Outline

The Book of Ruth is very short, consisting of only four chapters. The chapters are bookended with tragedy and death at the beginning and joy and birth at the end.

- Chapter 1: Naomi and her family leave Bethlehem and move to Moab, outside the Promised Land. Tragedy strikes multiple times, and Naomi releases her two widowed daughters-in-law from any responsibilities to her. Ruth refuses to leave the older woman and remains loyal to her.
- Chapter 2: Returning to Bethlehem, the two women look for food. Ruth meets Boaz, a farmer of noble character who respects the moral law, including caring for those in need. He offers to support the two women since he is related to Naomi (who is now called Mara).
- Chapter 3: Ruth meets Boaz again, and the two agree to marry. Boaz is in awe of Ruth's virtue.
- Chapter 4: Another relative has a closer tie to Naomi's family, but he passes on any marriage to Ruth. Boaz marries Ruth, and the two have a baby boy named Obed. The book concludes with a genealogy showing Obed to be the future King David's grandfather.

Application to Our Lives

In Ruth 1, Naomi is left widowed. Both of her sons have also died and left widows. Naomi shows herself to be a gracious mother-in-law and dispenses the two young widows of any responsibilities to her. One daughter-in-law jumps at the chance and leaves the older woman. Ruth, the other young woman, remains heroically loyal to Naomi. She even agrees to leave Moab, her own country, and move to the Promised Land of God's people (1:16).

Ruth is industrious, hard-working, and full of wisdom and virtue. She expects nothing and feels no entitlement, self-pity, or bitterness. She moves to Bethlehem and works to support her mother-in-law. God recognizes her goodness and blesses her. She is given a new family, a new land, a virtuous husband, and a son.

In the interactions within families, it periodically happens that mothers-in-law and daughters-in-law do not get along. Sometimes it's because of personality, temperament, miscommunication, or even jealousy or a closed heart. Whatever the cause, it can be hurtful to everyone involved.

The solution, of course, is virtue and a desire for goodness. This answer can be difficult, especially for the one who is offended or ostracized. And yet it's the answer. Imagine Ruth. She could have said, "Here I am, a widow, stuck with an older widow, away from my country and language, without food, farming in the heat!" She had a lot she could have complained about, but she didn't entertain such dark thoughts. She focused on the tasks at hand. She was virtuous and hard-working. And, because of her life, God blessed her. If she had given in to any bad thoughts or allowed her heart to go dark, God would not have blessed her so abundantly.

Basic Points

Author: The Jewish and Christian traditions attribute the Book of Ruth to the prophet Samuel, although several editors worked on the book through the ages.

Placement: Ruth is the eighth book of the Old Testament. It is part of what are called the historical books of the Bible. Ruth is a supplemental book of the principal narrative books of the Bible.

Keywords:

- Providence: God's fatherly care for his children.
- Widow: A woman whose husband has died. Widows were some of the most vulnerable, powerless people in the ancient world.
- Kinsman redeemer: The oldest unmarried man in a family, who is duty bound to marry a widow within his extended family. Boaz was the kinsman redeemer to Ruth.

Getting Started

With Ruth consisting of only four chapters, it is recommended that this heartwarming, powerful story be read in its entirety.

Concluding Prayer

O God,
you hear the cry of the orphan and the widow.
You are a Father to those in need.
You are a protector of the powerless.
You bless the virtuous.
Hear our cry.
Help us to be your instruments of service.
Strengthen us to show others your kindness.
Bless us with your grace.
Show us your mercy!
Through Christ our Lord.
Amen.

First Samuel

Then David said to the Philistine, "You come to me with a sword and with a spear and with a javelin; but I come to you in the name of the LORD of hosts, the God of the armies of Israel, whom you have defied."

1 SAMUEL 17:45

Opening Prayer
Gracious God,
you send us shepherds after your own heart.
You bless us and keep us.
Strengthen us.
Help us to know your way.
Give us the generosity to follow it.
Do not let us fall away from you.
Show us your face.
Through Christ our Lord.
Amen.

Basic Message
God blesses faithfulness and rejects pride. He seeks to lift up his people. For this to happen, however, we must be willing to accept his help.

Introductory Overview
The First Book of Samuel presents the rise of Samuel as a prophet of God's people, and his role in anointing Saul and David as the

first and second kings of the People of God. The book describes the downfall of Saul through his pride and the unexpected raising up of David because of his humility. The book explains the eventual establishment of the throne of King David.

Basic Outline
The First Book of Samuel consists of personal accounts of three men: Samuel, Saul, and David. The accounts form the internal structure of the book.

- Chapters 1–7: The birth, early life, prophetic call, and authority of the prophet Samuel.
- Chapters 8–15: The life, raising up, and tragic fall of King Saul.
- Chapters 16–31: The raising up, early life, and perils of King David.

Application to Our Lives
In First Samuel, chapter 17, a young David goes up against the giant Philistine, Goliath. The warrior was mocking the living God and the weakness and cowardice of the military of God's people. King Saul was in the rear of his army and uncertain what to do.

David was a shepherd boy. He had come to the camp to bring his brothers food rations. He hears the blasphemy of Goliath and offers to fight the giant. Since no soldier — including David's older brothers — will fight Goliath, the youthful David is sent out. Goliath is covered in armor. He looks like a human tank. David wears only a shepherd's tunic. As the raging warrior charges at David, the youth takes some stones from his pouch and uses his sling to pitch them at the enormous figure. The stones hit Goliath in the head and drop him dead.

The vulnerable David has won the day.

In our lives, there are many spiritual Goliaths that seek to scare us, overwhelm us, and charge in rage toward us. It is easy to succumb to their influence and allow dark spirits to fill our minds and hearts. There are many people who question their dignity, goodness, abilities, and capacity to deal with the duties, struggles, and surprises of their lives. In such moments, we don't need armor or more defense mechanisms. David declined Saul's armor before going to face Goliath (17:38–39). He didn't need it. It wouldn't have helped him. He needed to be true to himself and to who he was. He was a shepherd and so would use a shepherd's weapon. In our lives, we have to be true to ourselves, our strengths, and our weaknesses. We need to use the talents God has given us, trusting that he will see us through our trials one way or another. No Goliath need conquer us. We have what we need to conquer the burdens and struggles of life.

Basic Points

Author: The Jewish and Christian traditions attribute the First Book of Samuel to the prophet Samuel (and then Gad and Nathan, after Samuel's death), although several editors worked on the book through the ages.

Placement: First Samuel is the ninth book of the Old Testament. It is part of what are called the historical books of the Bible. First Samuel is the sixth of the principal narrative books of the Bible. (See Appendix A.)

Keywords:

- Philistine: An inhabitant of Philistia, located along the southwestern border of the Promised Land. The Philistines were a constant military threat to God's people. The Philistine worship of many gods regrettably influenced God's people.

- King: The king of God's people was God himself. When they asked to have a king like the other nations, the People of God offended God's sovereignty and their unique status as his people among all nations.

Getting Started

While the eventual goal is to read all thirty-one chapters of the First Book of Samuel, here are three selections that can get us started. Each selection shows us the depth and wisdom of First Samuel: Hannah's beautiful song of praise and prophecy (2:1–10); in spite of Saul's jealousy of David, David's friendship with Saul's son Jonathan and his marriage to Saul's daughter Michal (chapter 18); and David's act of mercy in sparing Saul's life because he respected and loved him, even though Saul had sought David's destruction (chapter 24).

Concluding Prayer

Eternal shepherd,
you never cease to care for us.
You protect and guide us.
You appoint leaders and bless them.
You are ever-watchful and all-loving.
You discipline and you console.
Bless us. Bless our leaders.
Through Christ our Lord.
Amen.

Second Samuel

When your days are fulfilled and you lie down with your fathers, I will raise up your offspring after you, who shall come forth from your body, and I will establish his kingdom. He shall build a house for my name, and I will establish the throne of his kingdom for ever. I will be his father and he shall be my son.

2 SAMUEL 7:12–14A

Opening Prayer

Everlasting Father,
you blessed the throne of David.
You have prepared your people.
The Son of David will come.
He will rule with justice forever.
He will bring peace to your people.
Come, Son of David.
Come, Lord Jesus!
Bring us redemption.
Spare us. Save us.
For you are Lord forever and ever.
Through Christ our Lord.
Amen.

Basic Message

God is faithful and fulfills his promises, in spite of our sins and fallenness.

Introductory Overview

The Second Book of Samuel describes the rule of King David, the problems of his governance over God's people, and the struggles within his family.

Basic Outline

The Second Book of Samuel consists of three major movements:

- Chapters 1–10: The successes and prosperity of King David.
- Chapters 11–20: The failures of King David and the rebellion against his authority.
- Chapters 21–24: The epilogue summarizing King David's life and expressing the hope for a future king.

Application to Our Lives

In Second Samuel, chapter 7, a prosperous King David recognizes that the Ark of the Covenant, which contains the presence of God on earth, is still in the tabernacle, the series of tents that surround the Ark. Being a man of devotion, David asks God if he might build him a temple. The request is sincere, as is God's answer.

God tells David no. He does not want the king to build him a house. Instead, God flips the request and tells David that *he* will build a house for *David*. The term *house* can mean a residence (or temple) as well as a lineage or dynasty. God means a lineage and tells David that David's throne — his house — will be blessed forever. One of his sons will sit on the throne forever.

This is an immense grace given to King David. It is a prominent prophecy, as God's people wait for the coming of the promised Savior. It is a blessing to David, who does not deserve it. Although king, David has told lies, stolen, deceived others, and committed adultery and murder. It seems as if David is far from God, yet David is a truly devout man who loves God. He has consistently repented and asked for mercy. He knows he needs God's pardon and peace. David is not perfect. But because of David's honesty and repentance, God blesses him abundantly.

In our lives, we have to identify the lies that sin and guilt try to convince us to believe. We have to be cautious about shame and self-hatred. We need to send them away, so that they have no power over us. Yes, we need to recognize our sins, but once we know them, we need to repent and let them go. God desires to take away our sins. He wants to bless us and show us our goodness. If we live in the constant darkness of old sin, we can never fully know the freedom of God's light and the joy of living a life with his blessings. No sin has the power to block God's blessings, unless we let it. God blessed David. He wants to bless us.

Basic Points

Author: The Jewish and Christian traditions attribute the Second Book of Samuel to the prophets Gad and Nathan, although several editors worked on the book through the ages.

Placement: Second Samuel is the tenth book of the Old Testament. It is part of what are called the historical books of the Bible. Second Samuel is the seventh of the principal narrative books of the Bible. (See Appendix A.)

Keywords:

- Throne of David: The popular expression used to describe God's blessing upon the lineage of King David. In particular, it refers to God's promise that a son of David will rule over God's people forever. The promise develops further the ancient promise of an

Anointed Savior. We now know that the Anointed Savior will come from Judah, will be of the House of David, and will sit on David's throne forever. These prophecies and promises are later fulfilled in Jesus Christ, son of Abraham, son of Judah, and son of David (see Mt 1:1).

- Absalom: The beloved son of King David who attempted to overthrow his father and take the throne for himself. Absalom's death is the lowest point in David's life and of his rule over God's people.

Getting Started

While the eventual goal is to read all twenty-four chapters of the Second Book of Samuel, here are three selections that can get us started. Each selection shows us the depth and wisdom of Second Samuel: the "Song of the Bow," David's eulogy for Saul and Jonathan (1:17–27); David's affair with Bathsheba, which led to murder (chapters 11–12); and David's grieving for his son Absalom, who betrayed him (chapter 18).

Concluding Prayer

Everlasting Father,
you rule from age to age.
You guide your people.
You prepare us for the Savior.
Sin has no power over you.
Your grace works through our fallenness.
You pour your mercy upon us.
Help us to see your presence.
Bless us! Save us!
Through Christ our Lord.
Amen.

First Kings

But he forsook the counsel which the old men gave him, and took counsel with the young men who had grown up with him and stood before him.

1 KINGS 12:8

Opening Prayer

Almighty and ever-living God,
you are the one true God,
glorious and triumphant.
Remove the idols from our hearts.
Take the false gods from our souls.
Show us your way.
Guide us. Strengthen us.
Help us to remain faithful to you.
Through Christ our Lord.
Amen.

Basic Message

Sin and idolatry have consequences. Such consequences affect us and those around us.

Introductory Overview

The First Book of Kings describes the rule of Solomon, the split of David's kingdom, and the initial line of kings in both the northern kingdom and the southern kingdom. In addition, the ministry of the prophets Elijah and Elisha are described in the book.

Basic Outline

The First Book of Kings has three main parts:

- Chapters 1–11: The rule of Solomon and the building of the Temple of Jerusalem.
- Chapters 12–14: The dividing of David's kingdom.
- Chapters 15–22: The succession of kings in the northern and southern kingdoms, and the ministry of Elijah and Elisha.

Application to Our Lives

In the First Book of Kings, chapter 12, we hear about Solomon's son Rehoboam, who becomes king when his father dies. When Rehoboam receives the crown, the people are angry about the heavy taxes he places upon them because of the royal building projects of King Solomon. A rebel leader, Jeroboam, comes back from Egypt and rallies the people against their new king.

Rehoboam, as a young king, is surrounded by older men of great wisdom. They counsel the new king, recommending that he serve the people, lighten the taxes, and show his love for them. Rehoboam, however, is displeased and disregards their counsel. Instead, he turns to his friends, who are as green and unseasoned as he is, and they tell him to chastise the people and impose even heavier taxes on them. The king listens, and the people revolt against him. This revolt leads to the eventual split of David's kingdom, which is one of the worst tragedies in salvation history.

In our lives, it can be difficult to ask for help and guidance. It can be even harder to listen to advice that might challenge us or cause us to show humility. If we desire to stop sin in its tracks and to heal division, we must listen to wisdom. Imagine if Rehoboam had listened to his advisers and shown deference to their wisdom. His kingdom would not have been divided, and God's people would have remained united and strong. In the decisions we make, we should always consult people of wisdom and show a willing heart to defer to them and accept their guidance.

Basic Points

Author: The Jewish and Christian traditions attribute the First Book of Kings to the prophet Jeremiah, although several editors worked on the book through the ages.

Placement: First Kings is the eleventh book of the Old Testament. It is part of what are called the historical books of the Bible. First Kings is the eighth of the principal narrative books of the Bible. (See Appendix A.)

Keywords:

- Temple of Jerusalem: The place of worship built by King Solomon. It housed the Ark of the Covenant, which held God's presence on earth. It was the center and heart of worship for God's people.
- Prophet: One who interceded for God's people and taught and defended the covenant of God. Prophets were not seers or fortunetellers. They were teachers, who admonished and called God's people to be faithful to the covenant God formed with them.

Getting Started

While the eventual goal is to read all twenty-two chapters of the First Book of Kings, here are three selections that can get us started. Each selection shows us the depth and wisdom of First Kings: the wisdom of Solomon and his decision regarding the true mother of a child (chapter 3); the dedication of the Temple of Jerusalem by King Solomon (chapter 8); and the prophet Elijah's resuscitation of a widow's son (17:17–24).

Concluding Prayer
Eternal Father,
you know all things.
You direct and guide all things.
You care for us and call us to yourself.
Help us to draw close to you.
Teach us your ways.
Show us your glory.
Through Christ our Lord.
Amen.

Second Kings

When they had crossed, Elijah said to Elisha, "Ask what I shall do for you, before I am taken from you." And Elisha said, "I beg you, let me inherit a double share of your spirit."

2 KINGS 2:9

Opening Prayer
Eternal God,
Lord and shepherd of your people,
you hear our cry as we turn to you.
Be the guardian of our souls.
Guide our hearts.
Keep us faithful to you.
Sustain us. Encourage us.
Show us your glory.
Through Christ our Lord.
Amen.

Basic Message
As we also hear in First Kings, God's loving plan for us cannot be destroyed by sin and rebellion.

Introductory Overview
The Second Book of Kings describes additional kings in both the northern kingdom and the southern kingdom. We also learn more about the ministry of the prophets Elijah and Elisha.

Basic Outline

The Second Book of Kings has four main parts:

- Chapters 1–8: The continuing story of Elijah and Elisha, including a series of kings in the northern and southern kingdoms.
- Chapters 9–16: A series of royal overthrows in the two kingdoms; the north and the south are weakened by infighting.
- Chapter 17: The fall of the northern kingdom to the Assyrians.
- Chapters 18–25: The last hopes for the southern kingdom, as good and bad kings continue to come and go. The southern kingdom falls to the Babylonians. Jerusalem and the Temple of Solomon are destroyed. A passing hope is given for the eventual restoration of David's house.

Application to Our Lives

In Second Kings, chapter 2, we hear about the passing of the great prophet Elijah. We're told that he rode into heaven in a chariot of fire. Because of this, he is considered the father of all prophets, as he was particularly blessed by God. Before entering eternity, however, Elijah spent time with his spiritual son and student, Elisha.

Elijah asked Elisha what he wanted before his teacher left this world. The younger prophet asked him for a double portion of his spirit. Elijah warned Elisha that he was asking for a hard gift, one that would come with great responsibilities. The gift was granted, and, true to the blessing, Elisha did double the miracles and signs of his teacher, so that he gave great service to God and his people.

In our lives, it's easy to seek only worldly blessings. With the challenges of life, we can think that more money, greater health, better relationships, and other things of this life are the be-all and end-all of our existence. Elisha, however, reminds us of greater and eternal things. It's important to seek closeness with God, wisdom, grace, and the power to remain faithful to God and have a loving spirit toward all people. As we seek to fulfill our responsibilities and be attentive to the things of this world, we need to put them in their proper place and keep our hearts on the things that are above.

Basic Points

Author: The Jewish and Christian traditions attribute the Second Book of Kings to the prophet Jeremiah, although several editors worked on the book through the ages.

Placement: Second Kings is the twelfth book of the Old Testament. It is part of what are called the historical books of the Bible. Second Kings is the ninth of the principal narrative books of the Bible. (See Appendix A.)

Keywords:

- Judah and Israel: The southern kingdom (Judah) and northern kingdom (Israel) after the tragic split of the kingdom of David.
- Babylonia: An ancient empire that once occupied the Promised Land of God's people, while sending them into exile for seventy years.

Getting Started

While the eventual goal is to read all twenty-five chapters of the Second Book of Kings, here are three selections that can get us started. Each selection shows us the depth and wisdom of Second Kings: the prophet Elisha's curing of Naaman, the Syrian general (5:1–19); the fall of the northern kingdom (Israel) to Assyria (chapter 17); and the rule of the righteous boy king, Josiah (chapters 22–23).

Concluding Prayer
Heavenly Father,
you protect and discipline,
you love and correct.
Help us to remain faithful to you.
Keep our hearts open to your instruction.
Guide us along your way.
Strengthen us. Console us.
Show us your glory.
Through Christ our Lord.
Amen.

First Chronicles

As the ark of the covenant of the LORD came to the city of David, Michal the daughter of Saul looked out of the window, and saw King David dancing and making merry; and she despised him in her heart.

1 CHRONICLES 15:29

Opening Prayer

All-holy God,
you dwell among your people.
You call us to holiness.
You desire to be our shepherd.
Help us to follow you.
We love you. Purify our love.
Strengthen us.
Help us to rejoice in your presence.
Through Christ our Lord.
Amen.

Basic Message

God has a plan for all of humanity. He is faithful to this plan, even when we are not. His plan perseveres through all the twists and turns of human pride and rebellion.

Introductory Overview

The First Book of Chronicles is the first part of a summary of salvation history from Adam, the first man, to the return of

God's people from the Babylonian Exile. As such, it repeats a lot
of previous content from First and Second Samuel and First and
Second Kings, although from a different perspective. The focus
of First Chronicles is the lineage and righteousness of David and
his preparations for the eventual Temple in Jerusalem.

Basic Outline
The First Book of Chronicles has two main parts:

- Chapters 1–9: A series of genealogies of David and
  the Levitical priesthood.
- Chapters 10–29: A series of stories about David that
  portray him as a symbol of the long-awaited Sav-
  ior-King.

Application to Our Lives
In the First Book of Chronicles, chapter 15, King David orders
the Ark of the Covenant to be brought to the new capital city,
Jerusalem (also called Zion). As an act of humility, David goes
himself to lead the Ark into the Holy City.

The Ark of the Covenant held the presence of God on earth.
Its care was restricted to the Levites. David respected this reserved service and called on the Levites to prepare themselves
spiritually for the task. As the Levites began to move the Ark,
festive music was played, and David himself, the anointed king
of God's people, danced before the Ark. He danced so joyfully
that his wife was embarrassed and hated him for being so spon-
taneous. David didn't care. The king's heart was full of awe and
wonder, delight and jubilation, exultation and triumph. He was
uplifted by the presence of God and was humbled to bring the
Ark into Jerusalem.

It is no wonder that the Bible tells us in several places that
King David had a heart for the Lord. In spite of his many sins, he

loved the Lord and sought to worship and please him.
In our lives, we are filled with heaviness and responsibilities.
We also have guilt over sins or shame over past actions. It can be
hard to be joyful. It's easy to let darkness and sorrow win. King
David, however, had a different approach to life: Repent of sin,
and rejoice in God's presence. This way of life is the right one
for us to follow. We can lift the heaviness, cast off the guilt and
shame, and be joyful. We can accept the love and mercy God
offers us. We can dance!

Basic Points

Author: The Jewish and Christian traditions attribute the First
Book of Chronicles to the priest Ezra, although several editors
worked on the book through the ages.

Placement: First Chronicles is the thirteenth book of the Old
Testament. It is part of what are called the historical books of the
Bible. First Chronicles is a supplemental book of the principal
narrative books of the Bible.

Keywords:

- Levites: The male members of the tribe of Levi, who
  were entrusted with the priesthood and its duties.
  They were consecrated to God by special prayers
  and were the only ones who were able to care for
  the Ark of the Covenant.
- Ephod: The garment worn by priests. It is unique
  that King David, who was not a Levite, wore an
  ephod (15:27). This action points to an eventual
  new priestly order, which will be held and fulfilled
  by Jesus Christ.

Getting Started

While the eventual goal is to read all twenty-nine chapters of the First Book of Chronicles, here are three selections that can get us started. Each selection shows us the depth and wisdom of First Chronicles: the holiness of the Ark of the Covenant and the death of Uzzah (chapter 13); the mistake of King David in calling for a census of God's people (chapter 21); and King David's dedication prayer for the Temple (29:10–22).

Concluding Prayer

Eternal Father,
King of kings and Lord of lords,
you bless us with hope.
You guide us and direct us.
Help us to worship you,
to love you,
to obey you.
Stay close to us.
Show us your glory.
Through Christ our Lord.
Amen.

Second Chronicles

Thus says Cyrus king of Persia, "The LORD, the God of heaven, has given me all the kingdoms of the earth, and he has charged me to build him a house at Jerusalem, which is in Judah. Whoever is among you of all his people, may the LORD his God be with him. Let him go up."

2 CHRONICLES 36:23

Opening Prayer
Good and gracious God,
you bless your people.
You call us to yourself.
You live among us.
You walk with us and lift us up.
Guide us with your grace.
Grant us your strength.
Through Christ our Lord.
Amen.

Basic Message
God has a plan for humanity, and we can learn about this plan by imitating the faithfulness and obedience of believers who lived before us.

Introductory Overview
The Second Book of Chronicles is the second part of a summary of salvation history from Adam, the first man, to the return of

God's people from the Babylonian Exile. As such, it repeats a lot of previous content from First and Second Samuel and First and Second Kings, although from a different perspective. The focus of Second Chronicles is the series of kings in the line of David who ruled the southern kingdom (Judah). It shows the blessings God gives to the faithful kings and the punishments the unfaithful ones receive.

Basic Outline
The Second Book of Chronicles has three main parts:

- Chapters 1–9: The preparations and the dedication of the Temple; Solomon's other accomplishments and his fame throughout the world.
- Chapters 10—36:14: A series of accounts of the kings of Judah.
- Chapter 36:15–23: The Babylonian Exile and Cyrus of Persia's edict for God's people to return home.

Application to Our Lives
In the Second Book of Chronicles, chapter 36, the pagan king Cyrus, ruler of Persia, receives instruction from the living God. Persia has overtaken Babylonia, and yet God's people are still in exile in his empire. After hearing from God, however, Cyrus obeys and allows God's people to return to Jerusalem.

Cyrus is hailed as the Lord's anointed (see Is 45:1). It's a specific title used for only a few people in salvation history. Each anointed one pointed God's people to the long-awaited Savior, *the* Anointed One. Cyrus was the only pagan to receive this significant title. It was given to him because he listened and obeyed, although previously he had not known, followed, or worshiped the living God.

In our lives, we must be careful not to restrict God's actions to only one group or state of affairs. God will work through anyone who listens to him, trusts him, and does as he asks. God had to work through Cyrus because so few of his own people listened to him. Our task is to remain open to God's working through any of his children, regardless of their status, affiliation, or associations. There are times in which God will speak through unexpected people, surprising circumstances, or peculiar means. We must always stay open to receiving God's words and wisdom — in whatever way he might choose to speak to us.

Basic Points

Author: The Jewish and Christian traditions attribute the Second Book of Chronicles to the priest Ezra, although several editors worked on the book through the ages.

Placement: Second Chronicles is the fourteenth book of the Old Testament. It is part of what are called the historical books of the Bible. Second Chronicles is a supplemental book of the principal narrative books of the Bible.

Keywords:

- Holy People: The call of God's people to be distinct from the other nations. God's people were to be distinguished by their justice and mercy.
- Glory of the Lord: A term used to refer to the presence of God.

Getting Started

While the eventual goal is to read all thirty-six chapters of the Second Book of Chronicles, here are three selections that can get us started. Each selection shows us the depth and wisdom of Second Chronicles: the bringing of the Ark of the Covenant into the Temple (chapter 5); the visit of the Queen of Sheba to King Solomon (9:1–12); and another account of the righteous King Josiah and the renewal of the covenant (chapters 34–35).

Concluding Prayer
Almighty Father,
you bless your people.
You guide us through our leaders.
Strengthen and sustain them.
Let them always obey your laws of goodness.
Let justice and kindness rule.
Show us your glory.
Through Christ our Lord.
Amen.

Ezra

Then arose Jeshua the son of Jozadak, with his fellow priests, and Zerubbabel the son of Shealtiel with his kinsmen, and they built the altar of the God of Israel, to offer burnt offerings upon it, as it is written in the law of Moses the man of God.

EZRA 3:2

Opening Prayer

Lord God,
protector of your people,
you restore what was lost,
you heal what was broken.
Time and time again,
you call us to yourself.
Give us your wisdom.
Keep us always in your grace.
Through Christ our Lord.
Amen.

Basic Message

God can heal what is broken and restore anything that is lost.

Introductory Overview

The Book of Ezra recounts the return of God's people to Jerusalem and the Promised Land of their forefathers. The book describes the building and dedication of the Second Temple, although the Ark of the Covenant was lost.

Basic Outline

The Book of Ezra has two main parts, centering on the key figures of Zerubbabel and Ezra:

- Chapters 1–6: Zerubbabel leads a wave of God's people back to the Promised Land and leads the building and dedication of the Second Temple.
- Chapters 7–10: Ezra leads another wave of God's people home and initiates a spiritual renewal among God's people.

Application to Our Lives

In Ezra 3, God's people have returned from their exile in Babylonia, and their worship according to the laws of Moses has been reinstated. When the people were taken into exile, it appeared as if all was lost. They had rebelled against God and broken his covenant, and then the Babylonians destroyed Jerusalem and the Temple.

Showing his perpetual faithfulness, God brought his people back home, renewed his covenant, and allowed for worship to begin again. This eventually led to the building of the Second Temple.

In our lives, when all hope seems lost, we need to rely on God's faithfulness. When things look broken, wayward, or without cause for encouragement, we can surrender our anxieties and fears to God and hope in him. Things may not always turn out the way we want, but they don't have to be as bad as we fear. As the remnant of God's people turned to him, God showed himself to be the healer and protector of his people. He also will be our healer and protector, if we will let him.

Basic Points

Author: The Jewish and Christian traditions attribute the Book of Ezra to the priest Ezra, although several editors worked on the book through the ages.

Placement: Ezra is the fifteenth book of the Old Testament. It is part of what are called the historical books of the Bible. Ezra is the tenth of the principal narrative books of the Bible. (See Appendix A.)

Keywords:

- Remnant: The small group of God's people who returned to the Promised Land and sought to live by God's covenant.
- Second Temple: In salvation history, there were only two Temple buildings: one built by Solomon and one by the exiles who returned to Jerusalem from Babylon. The Second Temple was an effort to rebuild what God had done through King Solomon, but the Ark of the Covenant was lost, and so the Second Temple never had the glory of Solomon's Temple. The definitive Temple in salvation history is Jesus Christ, who is the presence of God among us.
- Mixed marriage: The term used in Ezra for marriage between God's people and unbelievers. Ezra strongly denounced this practice in his spiritual reform.

Getting Started

Since the Book of Ezra has only ten chapters and contains the essential, challenging event of God's people returning to the Promised Land after a seventy-year exile in Babylon, it is recommended that the book be read in its entirety.

Concluding Prayer
Burning fire,
Love above all loves,
show us your presence.
Grant us renewal.
We turn to you.
We worship you. We love you.
Show us your glory.
Through Christ our Lord.
Amen.

Nehemiah

*Thus I cleansed them from everything foreign,
and I established the duties of the priests and
Levites, each in his work; and I provided for the
wood offering, at appointed times, and for the first
fruits. Remember me, O my God, for good.*

NEHEMIAH 13:30–31

Opening Prayer
O God,
who are great, mighty, and awesome,
hear our prayer.
Help us to draw close to you.
Grant us wisdom.
Help us to reform.
Guide our efforts.
Bless us with your wisdom.
Keep us always in your grace.
Through Christ our Lord.
Amen.

Basic Message
Programs and human effort alone are not sufficient for spiritual reform. We must have a new heart.

Introductory Overview
The Book of Nehemiah recounts the rebuilding of the walls of

Jerusalem and the efforts of Nehemiah and Ezra to bring about a greater faithfulness to God's covenant.

Basic Outline
The Book of Nehemiah has three main parts:

- Chapters 1–7: The account of Nehemiah's rebuilding of the walls of Jerusalem.
- Chapters 8–12: Nehemiah and Ezra lead God's people to a recommitment to the covenant.
- Chapter 13: The repeated disobedience of God's people and Nehemiah's anger and punishment of the people.

Application to Our Lives
In Nehemiah 13, Nehemiah realizes that all his efforts at spiritual reform have fallen on deaf ears and wayward hearts. God's people have not responded to his efforts to foster greater faithfulness to the covenant God has made with them.

Nehemiah has given his entire life to reforming God's people. He has taken a risk in asking the Persian king to allow him to go home — to rebuild the walls of Jerusalem and bring God's people back to their spiritual senses. Seeing his efforts dismissed by his own people, he could have fallen into deep sorrow or melancholy. He could have been consumed by self-pity and entitlement. Instead, Nehemiah turns to prayer. He asks God to remember his good efforts. He surrenders all his work to God. He trusts that God would bless his efforts at a future time.

In our lives, when we see our efforts ignored, dismissed, or mocked, we can get angry, blame others, refuse kindness, and turn away from God. We can accuse God of not helping us and can seek revenge on those who have hurt our efforts. Nehemiah shows us a different way. We can work hard and then offer up our work to God. He is the one who blesses it at the right time. If we labor and forget God, he cannot bless us. If we work hard and surrender all things to God, then we are victorious no matter what the immediate outcome might be. Nehemiah understood this truth. So can we.

Basic Points

Author: The Jewish and Christian traditions attribute the Book of Nehemiah to Nehemiah, although several editors worked on the book through the ages.

Placement: Nehemiah is the sixteenth book of the Old Testament. It is part of what are called the historical books of the Bible. Nehemiah is the eleventh of the principal narrative books of the Bible. (See Appendix A.)

Keywords:

- Festival of Booths: The ancient feast described by Moses in which God's people remembered their time in the desert. During its historical observance, people lived outside, and there was a blessing of water. The feast was unobserved for generations until it was restored after the Babylonian Exile.

Getting Started

While the eventual goal is to read all thirteen chapters of the Book of Nehemiah, here are three selections that can get us started. Each selection shows us the depth and wisdom of Nehemiah: Nehemiah's sorrow over his people and his bold request (2:1–10); the celebration of the ancestral Festival of Booths (8:13–18); and the national confession of God's people and the renewal of the covenant (chapter 9).

Concluding Prayer

Eternal God,
Lord of all the nations,
you call us to worship you.
You lift us up out of our fallenness.
You show us your mercy.
Hear our plea. Come to us.
Help us to worship you.
Guide us in loving you.
Strengthen us to serve you.
Through Christ our Lord.
Amen.

Tobit

I did not believe her, and told her to return it to the owners; and I blushed for her. Then she replied to me, "Where are your charities and your righteous deeds? You seem to know everything!"

Tobit 2:14

Opening Prayer
Father of all,
you send us your angels.
They serve as guides and healers.
Keep us safe from harm.
Help us to see your presence.
Show us your providence.
Through Christ our Lord.
Amen.

Basic Message
God is present among us. He tests us and responds to our prayers with protection and blessings.

Introductory Overview
The Book of Tobit is a historical novel that shows a glimpse of the life of God's people under Assyrian control. It depicts the struggles and persecutions of Tobit, who seeks to do the will of God, and the journey of his son, Tobias, as he goes to collect a debt for his father. The young man's adventure includes an an-

gelic guide, a marriage, an exorcism, a festive homecoming, the healing of Tobit, and a song of praise and thanksgiving to God.

Basic Outline
The Book of Tobit has three movements:

- Chapters 1–3: The situations in Nineveh and Ecbatana.
- Chapters 4–12: Tobias's journey and adventures.
- Chapter 13–14: Tobit's song of praise and parting wisdom.

Application to Our Lives
In Tobit 2, we find a biblical account of a full, all-out marital fight. After Tobit was unexpectedly blinded after performing a righteous act, his wife, Anna, took on some work to support her family. Her various weaving work brought in some much-needed money. In the meantime, Tobit was feeling sorry for himself. He was blind and unable to work.

On one occasion, Anna is given a small goat along with her wages. The extra gift indicates how excellent she is at her craft. When she returns home, Tobit hears the bleating of the goat. He is angered, assuming that his wife stole the goat. He tells her to return it. Anna replies that the goat was not stolen but given to her as extra payment for her work. Tobit dismisses his wife's comments and demands that she return the goat. Anna is surprised and asks Tobit where his righteous deeds are now. Tobit repents and turns to prayer (3:1–6).

The account between Tobit and Anna is both dramatic and intense. It's a true fight between spouses. Thanks be to God, it ends well. For those who are married, disagreements and fights happen. They can be passing arguments or fierce disputes. In such situations, both spouses need to be committed to truth and reconciliation in the Lord. Anna would not accept being called a thief by her husband. Tobit heard and accepted that his righteousness (which caused his blindness) was not — in turn — being shown to his wife. Both accepted the truth, even in the midst of an argument. Spouses today are called to approach their fights and disagreements with the same deference and love for truth.

Basic Points

Author: The Jewish and Christian traditions attribute the Book of Tobit to Tobit, although the historical nature of the person is now questioned.

Placement: Tobit is the seventeenth book of the Old Testament. It is part of what are called the historical books of the Bible. Tobit is a supplemental book of the principal narrative books of the Bible. Tobit is also one of the deuterocanonical books. (See Appendix B.)

Keywords:

- Angels and archangels: Spiritual beings who serve God. They have specific tasks, such as healing, protecting, and delivering messages. Tobias is befriended by the archangel Raphael.
- Samaria: The capital of the northern kingdom (Israel). Because of the city's prominence, the residents of the northern kingdom were eventually called Samaritans. Tobit and his family originally lived in Samaria. They were relocated by the occupying Assyrian military to Nineveh.

Getting Started

The Book of Tobit is a historical novel of fourteen chapters. As such, it has a smooth pace and can be a quick read. It's recommended that the book be read in its entirety. If that's not possible, here are three selections that can get us started. Each selection shows us the depth and wisdom of Tobit: Tobit's righteous act of burying the dead (1:16–22); the angel Raphael accompanies Tobias on his journey (chapter 5); and the exorcism of an evil spirit and the joy of married love (chapter 8).

Concluding Prayer
Heavenly Father,
you journey with your people.
You are our companion and shepherd.
Watch over us.
Accompany us.
Protect us.
Heal us.
Through Christ our Lord.
Amen.

Judith

Judith said to them, "Listen to me. I am about to do a thing which will go down through all generations of our descendants."

JUDITH 8:32

Opening Prayer
Lord God,
Father of widows,
Protector of your people,
hear our cry as we turn to you.
Come to our aid.
Rescue us from our distress.
Free us from evil.
Through Christ our Lord.
Amen.

Basic Message
God protects his people. He humbles the proud and arrogant and raises up the humble and weak.

Introductory Overview
The Book of Judith is a historical novel that shows the resistance of God's people to an invading army (possibly the Assyrians). The resistance is led by Judith, a daring and beautiful widow who wants to defend her people and show the strength of God's people to the nations.

Basic Outline
The Book of Judith has two main parts:

- Chapters 1–7: The historical and political situation of the time.
- Chapters 8–16: Judith, her actions, and their noble results.

Application to Our Lives
In Judith 8, we are given a brief background on this great woman of the Bible. We are told that Judith's husband died of heat exhaustion during the barley season, but that he left her with great wealth. We are also told of her beauty, stamina, and strength. After our passing introduction, we read how Judith challenges the elders for their weakness and fear.

Judith recalls events in salvation history and calls on the people to carry on this inheritance of faith and fortitude. She then steps up and tells the elders and the people that she will do something that will be recorded for ages to come. Although no one could have expected it, Judith is speaking about how she will outwit and execute Holofernes, the general of the army threatening God's people.

The account is shocking in itself, but it also stands out that the hero of the story is a widow. In the ancient world, widows were a vulnerable class of people. They were often taken advantage of and dismissed. In this account, though, a widow — the least likely of candidates — is the savior and guardian of her people.

In our lives, we should not be surprised when the least likely among us are the ones chosen by God for a specific task and mission. It is tried-and-true biblical wisdom that God will raise up the humble and cast down the proud. As such, we should always follow the path of humility, saying yes to whatever is asked of us and accepting when others are asked instead of us.

Basic Points

Author: The Jewish and Christian traditions attribute the Book of Judith to Judith, although the historical nature of the person is now questioned.

Placement: Judith is the eighteenth book of the Old Testament. It is part of what are called the historical books of the Bible. Judith is a supplemental book of the principal narrative books of the Bible and is also one of the deuterocanonical books. (See Appendix B.)

Keywords:

- Nebuchadnezzar: Although identified as the king of the Assyrians in the Book of Judith, the name is most commonly associated with the infamous ruler of Babylon.
- Self-defense/just war: The virtuous use of reasonable and proportionate force in protecting our personal safety or the safety of our homeland. In taking Holofernes's life, Judith was protecting her well-being and her homeland.

Getting Started

The Book of Judith is a historical novel of sixteen chapters. As such, it has a smooth pace and can be a quick read. It's recommended that the book be read in its entirety. If that's not possible, here are three selections that can get us started. Each selection shows us the depth and wisdom of Judith: the repentance and prayers of God's people (4:8–15); Judith's beheading of the Assyrian general who threatened the safety of God's people (13:1–10); and the song of praise of Judith and God's people (16:1–17).

Concluding Prayer

Almighty God,
Father of justice,
Strength of the vulnerable,
you choose the humble of the earth.
You raise up leaders to defend your people.
Protect us. Defend us from evil.
Bless us.
Through Christ our Lord.
Amen.

Esther

And who knows whether you have not come
to the kingdom for such a time as this?

ESTHER 4:14B

Opening Prayer
Eternal God,
Lord above all lords,
you choose the leaders of your people.
You call us to yourself.
You give us strength to do what is right.
You bless us and protect us.
Show us your presence.
Through Christ our Lord.
Amen.

Basic Message
God watches over and protects his people.

Introductory Overview
The Book of Esther is a historical novel that depicts God's people living under Persian control. The story is about Hadassah (Esther) and Mordecai, both of whom are members of God's people. Esther is made Queen of Persia, and Mordecai — after some royal twists and turns — becomes a powerful court official. Both of them use their influence to save God's people from persecution.

Basic Outline

The Book of Esther has four movements:

- Chapters 1–2: The feasts of the king of Persia and the selection of Esther.
- Chapter 3: The decree against God's people.
- Chapters 4–8: Esther's bravery and request to the king.
- Chapters 9–10: The saving triumph of God's people, and the institution of the feast of Purim.

Application to Our Lives

In Esther 4, Esther hears about the edict against God's people. She has to decide whether to say something. By Persian law, however, she could be executed for going before the king without being summoned. The king has already replaced the previous queen with Esther. Times are uncertain, and her decision could have capital importance, for herself and God's people. As Esther is discerning what to do, her cousin and foster father, Mordecai, tells her that salvation would come for God's people, and that perhaps she has been made queen precisely for this moment.

Mordecai's observation about Esther forms the backbone of the entire book. God's providence made Esther the queen. There had been moral compromise and much sin, and God's people were in exile, but God's loving care for his people had moved and worked through everything to put Esther on the throne, where she could advocate for and defend God's people.

In our lives, there are times when we see moral compromise, accommodation to evil, great sin, and darkness. We can feel as if everything good has somehow been sent into exile. And yet we are reminded by the story of Esther that God can — and does — work in and through dark and dangerous situations. God will raise up good people, he will grant blessings and opportunities, and he will seek to protect and care for his people, no matter what the state of affairs might be. God's power is mightier than any evil. His light is stronger than any darkness.

Basic Points

Author: The Jewish and Christian traditions attribute the Book of Esther to Esther and Mordecai, although the historical nature of these persons is now questioned.

Placement: Esther is the nineteenth book of the Old Testament. It is part of what are called the historical books of the Bible. Esther is a supplemental book of the principal narrative books of the Bible.

Keywords:

- Persia: The ancient empire that conquered the Babylonian Empire. Cyrus of Persia allowed God's people to return to the Promised Land. Some of God's people, such as Esther and Mordecai, remained in Persia.
- Purim: The feast honoring the protection of God's people during the reign of Queen Esther of Persia.
- ABC: A simple way of remembering the three early empires that either occupied, exiled, or controlled God's people — namely, the Assyrians, the Babylonians, and Cyrus of Persia.

Getting Started

The Book of Esther is a historical novel of ten chapters. As such, it has a smooth pace and can be a quick read. It's recommended that the book be read in its entirety. If that's not possible, here are three selections that can get us started. Each selection shows us the depth and wisdom of Esther: Esther's decision to help God's people (chapter 4); Esther's boldness for God's people (7:1–5); and the destruction of the enemies of God's people (9:1–17).

Concluding Prayer

Most Holy God,
you protect and ransom your people.
You never allow darkness to win.
You send us the Light of Truth.
Bless us with wisdom.
Strengthen us with your grace.
Help us to do your will.
Cast out fear.
Show us your presence.
Through Christ our Lord.
Amen.

First Maccabees

*Now, my children, show zeal for the law, and give
your lives for the covenant of our fathers.*

1 MACCABEES 2:50

Opening Prayer
O God,
you correct and defend your people.
You are the hammer against evil.
Help us to turn to you.
Enlighten our minds.
Strengthen our wills.
Fortify our hearts to do your will.
Show us your presence.
Through Christ our Lord.
Amen.

Basic Message
God is with those who fight for righteousness.

Introductory Overview
The First Book of Maccabees describes the Greek occupation of
the Promised Land and the military efforts of the Maccabees to
rid the land of Greek influences and restore the covenant of God.

Basic Outline
The First Book of Maccabees centers on six main people:

- Chapter 1: Antiochus Epiphanes and his suppression of God's people.
- Chapter 2: Mattathias the priest and his revolt.
- Chapters 3–9:22: Judas Maccabeus and his military efforts.
- Chapters 9:23—12: Jonathan, the high priest and his acts as statesman.
- Chapters 13–16:17: Simon and the beginnings of the new monarchy.
- Chapter 16:18—24: John Hyrcanus I and the continuing work of the Maccabees.

Application to Our Lives

In First Maccabees 2, the priest Mattathias witnesses the sacrilege and blasphemy of the Greeks and those who followed them. He is outraged by their offenses and their disregard for the covenant of God and the traditions of God's people. In his sorrow and anger, he turns to prayer. He cries out to God and does penance.

When the Greeks, however, come to Mattathias's town and call on him, precisely as an elder of God's people, to offer false worship, Mattathias refuses and gives full vent to his righteous anger in defense of God's covenant. This begins the Maccabean Revolt. After some initial battles, when Mattathias is about to die, he calls on his five sons to continue his work and to give their lives in defense of the covenant of their forefathers.

In our lives, we can learn from Mattathias to respond to evil and wickedness with prayer and penance. Mattathias did not intend to launch a revolt. In many respects, it was forced upon him. He sought to pray and do penance for his people because he knew their weakness but also their potential for righteousness. Even after other actions were required of him, he knew that the highest and most noble response was prayer and penance. In the difficulties of our lives, it's easy to get angry and to justify fighting evil with evil. We must therefore begin with prayer. We must seek divine guidance and do only what is expected of us. Our good work must first be a spiritual response.

Basic Points

Author: The Jewish and Christian traditions attribute the First Book of Maccabees to John Hyrcanus I, although its author was more likely a court historian of the same time period.

Placement: First Maccabees is the twentieth book of the Old Testament. It is part of what are called the historical books of the Bible. First Maccabees is the twelfth of the principal narrative books of the Bible. (See Appendix A.) First Maccabees is also one of the deuterocanonical books. (See Appendix B.)

Keywords:

- Hellenization: The movement to promote Greek learning and culture throughout the world. It was considered a sign of progress and enlightenment and was used to violate the covenant of God. It was the reason for the revolt of the Maccabees.
- Hasmonean dynasty: The lineage of kings of the independent kingdom of Israel who were descendants of the Maccabees.

Getting Started

While the eventual goal is to read all sixteen chapters of the First Book of Maccabees, here are three selections that can get us started. Each selection shows us the depth and wisdom of First Maccabees: the sorrow of Mattathias over the idolatry in Jerusalem (2:1–14); the rededication of the Second Temple and the feast of Hanukkah (4:36–59); and the beginning of the Hasmonean dynasty (14:25–49).

Concluding Prayer

All-holy God,
you summon us to yourself.
You call us to worship.
Purify our hearts.
Strengthen our resolve.
Help us to love you above all things.
Through Christ our Lord.
Amen.

Second Maccabees

Do not fear this butcher, but prove worthy of your brothers. Accept death, so that in God's mercy I may get you back again with your brothers.

2 MACCABEES 7:29

Opening Prayer
Eternal Father,
you formed us in your own image.
You call us to worship you,
so that we can know our dignity.
Remove all false worship from our hearts.
Help us to turn to you.
Teach us your way of love.
Fortify our hearts to do your will.
Show us your glory.
Through Christ our Lord.
Amen.

Basic Message
As we see in First Maccabees, God is with those who fight for righteousness.

Introductory Overview
The Second Book of Maccabees gives a dramatic retelling of some of the stories contained in First Maccabees. It emphasizes the nobility of righteous suffering and martyrdom.

Basic Outline

The Second Book of Maccabees consists of five main parts, centering on three prominent figures:

- Chapters 1–2: Introduction with two letters from Jerusalem to Alexandria, Egypt.
- Chapter 3: The rule of Seleucus IV Philopator.
- Chapters 4–10:8: The rule of Antiochus IV Epiphanes.
- Chapters 10:9—15:36: The rule of Antiochus V Eupator.
- Chapter 15:37–39: Epilogue.

Application to Our Lives

In Second Maccabees 7, a mother and seven brothers are arrested for refusing to eat pork. At the time, abstaining from pork was part of God's law, and God's people were expected to observe it. But such religious observance violated the king's decrees, which were meant to make God's people more like the Greeks, who worshiped many false gods.

The king imposes a harsh torture upon the brothers. Each brother — one after the other — accepts such violence and declares his trust in and love for the living God as he endures martyrdom for the sake of God's law.

After the death of the sixth brother, the seventh one — who has witnessed the torture and death of his older brothers — is promised great riches and public office if he will break God's law and follow his earthly king. As such things are being spoken to him, his mother calls him to faithfulness and tells him to die nobly and in the spirit of his brothers. The young man refuses wealth and public office and accepts martyrdom. He is tortured the worst of all. Shortly afterward, his mother is also martyred.

In our lives, it can be difficult to speak the truth to our loved ones. It can be hard for parents to give testimony or offer correction to their adult children who are away from the Faith or are in grave sin. The mother of the seven sons gives us all a witness. She trusted in the reward of paradise and placed that above all things. There was no room in her heart for human respectability, worldly vanity, or compromise. The stakes were too high. In a similar fashion, we must speak the truth in love to our family members. We must give witness to truth and right living.

Basic Points

Author: The Jewish and Christian traditions attribute the Second Book of Maccabees to John Hyrcanus I, although its author was more likely a court historian of the same time period.

Placement: Second Maccabees is the twenty-first book of the Old Testament. It is part of what are called the historical books of the Bible. Second Maccabees is a supplemental book of the principal narrative books of the Bible. Second Maccabees is also one of the deuterocanonical books. (See Appendix B.)

Keywords:

- High priest: The chief priest of the Temple. He was the coordinator of worship and the spiritual voice of God's people.
- Prayers for the dead: The noble practice of offering sacrifices and other prayers for the purification of the dead.

Getting Started

While the eventual goal is to read all fifteen chapters of the Second Book of Maccabees, here are three selections that can get us started. Each selection shows us the depth and wisdom of Second Maccabees: the strength of the elderly Eleazar in refusing to violate the dietary laws of God (6:18–31); the repentance of the dying Antiochus IV Epiphanes, as he acknowledges that only God is God (9:1–12); and the prayers and expiation for the dead (12:38–45).

Concluding Prayer
Almighty God and Father,
hear our plea.
Destroy the forces of evil.
Scatter all darkness.
Remember us.
Remember our beloved dead.
Bless those who serve you.
Help us to love you above all things.
Through Christ our Lord.
Amen.

Wisdom Books

Job
Psalms
Proverbs
Ecclesiastes
Song of Solomon
Wisdom*
Sirach*

---

*A deuterocanonical book. (See Appendix B.)

Job

I had heard of you by the hearing of the ear,
but now my eye sees you.

JOB 42:5

Opening Prayer

All-loving Father,
your beautiful creation is fallen.
We have introduced sin
and brought chaos with us.
Suffering is now our state,
a consequence of our sin.
Help us. Do not abandon us.
Allow our suffering to be redeemed.
Give us hope.
Show us your glory.
Through Christ our Lord.
Amen.

Basic Message

God is just and good, even though there is suffering and evil in the world.

Introductory Overview

The Book of Job is a poetic story that describes the hardships of Job, a righteous and good man who undergoes great suffering. The book recounts several conversations about justice and why good people suffer. It concludes with God speaking to Job about divine wisdom and power.

Basic Outline

The Book of Job consists of four parts:

- Chapters 1–2: Introduction of Job and his hardships.
- Chapters 3–37: Multiple conversations between Job and four friends about the justice of God and evil in the world.
- Chapters 38–41: God's revelation and response to Job.
- Chapters 42: Epilogue.

Application to Our Lives

In Job 38–42, God responds to Job's complaints and the supposed wisdom of his friends. In contrast to their claims about justice, God has revealed to Job his divine power and wisdom. He has demonstrated that humanity does not have sufficient knowledge or experience to make any claim about justice. No one was with God when he created the world or ordered its existence or brought forth mighty creatures. No human being has any legitimate claim to justice, since our perspective is narrow and limited.

In response, Job repents. He tells God that he has heard about him in the past, but now he has seen him. The testimony of others was important, but now he has had his own encounter with God. Such an encounter makes all the difference. Job accepts the ways of God and wants to be more trusting.

In our lives, we hear a lot about God. There are many voices and perspectives about God. Through it all, however, God has revealed himself. He desires for us to see him, to know him personally. This encounter can come through the sacraments, through the reading of the Bible, or through personal prayer. While we need the witness of others, it cannot overshadow our own experience of God. We each need to hear — but also see — the living God.

Basic Points

Author: The Jewish and Christian traditions attribute the Book of Job to Job, although the historical nature of the person is questioned by some scholars today.

Placement: Job is the twenty-second book of the Old Testament. It is part of what are called the wisdom books of the Bible. Job is a supplemental book of the principal narrative books of the Bible.

Keywords:

- Leviathan and Behemoth: Two creatures referenced by God in his conversation with Job. Possibly dinosaurs or references to mythological creatures, the massive sea and land animals represent the gravity of God's power and the perplexity of creation.
- Fallen world: The theological term to describe creation after the Fall from grace by our first parents. Because of the Fall, creation and our human nature now experience evil and suffering.

Getting Started

The Book of Job is a poetic book of forty-two chapters. It reads very quickly, even though some of the points require deeper reflection. The recommendation, therefore, is that the book be read in its entirety, as we might read a novel. If this approach is not possible, then here are three selections that can get us started. Each selection shows us the depth and wisdom of Job: God's judgment to allow Job to suffer (2:1–10); Elihu's explanation of suffering and his defense of God (chapters 34–37); and God's discourse to Job and the disclosure of his wisdom and power (chapters 38–41).

Concluding Prayer

Almighty Father,
Creator of all things,
Your providence guides all things
and makes them beautiful.
We introduced sin and chaos into our world.
Help us with your grace.
Give us your strength.
Accept our sufferings.
Show us your glory.
Through Christ our Lord.
Amen.

Psalms

Blessed is the man
*   who walks not in the counsel of the wicked,*
nor stands in the way of sinners,
*   nor sits in the seat of scoffers;*
but his delight is in the law of the LORD,
*   and on his law he meditates day and night.*

PSALM 1:1–2

Opening Prayer
Everlasting Father,
we reflect on your teachings.
We contemplate your wisdom.
We seek your face.
We praise you. We bless you.
We adore you. We love you.
Turn to us.
Help us to delight in you.
Accept our adoration.
Hear our cry.
Through Christ our Lord.
Amen.

Basic Message
God is worthy of our complete praise and thanksgiving.

Introductory Overview

The Book of Psalms is a collection of 150 poems, songs, and prayers based upon reflections on the teachings of God. The Book of Psalms is popularly called the "hymnbook" of the Jerusalem Temple, since the psalms were composed for music and used for worship in Jerusalem.

Note: In the Book of Psalms, there are no chapters. Each psalm, regardless of its length, is treated as only one "chapter." The verses are still given as small numbers within each psalm.

Basic Outline

The Book of Psalms consists of seven main parts:

- Psalms 1–2: Introductory Psalms.
- Psalms 3–41: First Book of Psalms.
- Psalms 42–72: Second Book of Psalms.
- Psalms 73–89: Third Book of Psalms.
- Psalms 90–106: Fourth Book of Psalms.
- Psalms 107–145: Fifth Book of Psalms.
- Psalms 146–150: Concluding Psalms.

Application to Our Lives

In Psalm 1, the psalmist sings that those who meditate on the law of God find delight. This observation is an introduction to the entire book. As God's people reflect on his teachings, they will find peace and joy. And so, as there are five Books of Moses, the psalms are divided into five books.

As God's people reflect on Divine Revelations, teachings, and the moral law of God, they will be led to prayer, song, and true worship. Such a movement of the heart indicates that the ways of God are not solely about the moral law; they are about a relationship with God and an abundance of life.

In our lives, we have to be cautious not to make the teach-

ings of God only about moral truth. The moral way of life is
needed for us as children of God, but it is meant to lead us to
greater virtue, prayer, song, and adoration of God. The moral law
is not an end in itself. It is tempting to turn our own relationship
with God into a mere moral code, which we think we can control
and sometimes even impose upon other people. Our relationship with God — while it contains the moral law — is something
much greater and far more abundant than just a set of moral dos
and don'ts. We are called to find delight in God, to rejoice, and to
know his love and kindness in our lives.

Basic Points

Author: The Jewish and Christian traditions attribute the Book
of Psalms to King David, who wrote or collected the various poems, songs, and prayers that the book comprises.

Placement: Psalms is the twenty-third book of the Old Testament. It is part of what are called the wisdom books of the Bible.
Psalms is a supplemental book of the principal narrative books
of the Bible.

Keywords:

- Psalms of lament: One of the major designations
  within the Book of Psalms. These psalms express
  anger and confusion over evil, suffering, or hard-
  ship. They are often filled with sorrow and include
  petitions for deliverance and consolation.
- Psalms of praise: One of the major designations
  within the Book of Psalms. These psalms express
  hope, joy, and festivity over blessings, victories, and
  the goodness of life. They are often filled with jubilation and words of triumph.

Getting Started

The Book of Psalms is a collection of 150 poems, songs, and prayers. As such, it is an easy book to read in small portions. The goal, however, is to eventually read the book in its entirety. In the meantime, here are five selections that can get us started. Each selection shows us the depth and wisdom of Psalms: the beloved "shepherd's psalm" (Psalm 23); King David's powerful psalm of repentance after he committed adultery (Psalm 51); the psalm of God's priest-king, which is the most cited psalm in the New Testament (Psalm 110); the Hallel Psalms, or "psalms of praise" (Psalms 113–118); and the psalm of God's glory, often called the "alphabet psalm," since its petitions follow the letters of the Hebrew alphabet. This is the longest psalm in the book (Psalm 119).

Concluding Prayer

All-powerful, glorious God,
Joy of our ancestors,
Glory to the nations,
Hope of your people,
we praise you!
You are the beginning and the end of all things.
Your grace is triumphant,
Your love is everlasting!
We praise you!
Give us your strength.
Help us to rejoice in your teachings.
Fill us with your Spirit.
Show us your glory!
For you are Lord forever and ever.
Through Christ our Lord.
Amen.

Proverbs

Strength and dignity are her clothing,
  and she laughs at the time to come.
She opens her mouth with wisdom,
  and the teaching of kindness is on her tongue.

PROVERBS 31:25–26

Opening Prayer
Eternal wisdom,
source of all that is true,
enlighten our minds.
Open our hearts.
Instruct us in your ways.
Show us your goodness.
Help us to rejoice in your beauty.
Through Christ our Lord.
Amen.

Basic Message
God is the source of all wisdom. Reverence for God is the beginning of wisdom in the human heart.

Introductory Overview
The Book of Proverbs is a collection of speeches, poetry, and maxims that teach or reinforce wisdom and the path of righteousness.

Note: In the Book of Proverbs, there are no chapters. Each

proverb, regardless of its length, is treated as only one "chapter." The verses are still given as small numbers within each proverb.

Basic Outline

The Book of Proverbs consists of three main parts:

- Proverbs 1–9: Introduction to the way of wisdom.
- Proverbs 10–29: Collections of various maxims.
- Proverbs 30–31: Conclusion and the witness of wise people.

Application to Our Lives

As the Book of Proverbs begins with a father's wisdom to his son, so, in parallel form, it concludes with a mother's wisdom to her son. In Proverbs 31, therefore, we are told of King Lemuel and the wisdom his mother passes on to him. In particular, she stresses the traits of a strong leader and the attributes of a godly woman who lives by wisdom.

The section of Proverbs 31 that describes a holy woman is an "alphabet poem," since each stanza begins with a letter of the Hebrew alphabet. Such an artistic structure is done on purpose, so as to reflect the importance of wisdom in every part of life, from marriage and family to work, business, and community life. Thus, the righteous woman conducts all her affairs with wisdom.

In our lives, we need to seek wisdom and its guidance. We are also called to pursue righteousness in all the parts of our lives. Each of us, men and women alike, need to humble ourselves and ask God for his instruction. We need to approach the supposed wisdom of our fallen world with a healthy suspicion. We were made for divine wisdom. It helps us to deal with the struggles of this life and not be overwhelmed by them. We need to turn to God. We need his wisdom.

Basic Points

Author: The Jewish and Christian traditions attribute the Book of Proverbs to King Solomon, who wrote or collected the various speeches, poems, and maxims that the book comprises.

Placement: Proverbs is the twenty-fourth book of the Old Testament. It is part of what are called the wisdom books of the Bible. Proverbs is a supplemental book of the principal narrative books of the Bible.

Keywords:

- Wisdom: Unlike contemporary definitions, the biblical definition of *wisdom* is much more holistic. *Wisdom* is understood as a learned, practical skill that helps a person to live virtuously through a holy reverence for God and truth.
- Parental guidance: The responsibility of parents to pass on wisdom to their children. This obligation is strongly emphasized in the Book of Proverbs.

Getting Started

The Book of Proverbs is a collection of thirty-one proverbs consisting of speeches, poems, and maxims. As such, it is an easy book to read in small portions. The goal, however, is to eventually read the book in its entirety. In the meantime, here are three selections that can get us started. Each selection shows us the depth and wisdom of Proverbs: the creation and place of wisdom in creation (8:22–36); an example of a collection of maxims (chapter 20); and the witness of Agur on the importance of the Bible (chapter 30).

Concluding Prayer
Eternal Father,
Fount of wisdom,
Ocean of righteousness,
Hear our plea.
Teach us your truth.
Guide us along the path of goodness.
Show us your beauty.
Convert our hearts.
Open our minds.
Instruct us. Guide us.
Show us your glory!
Through Christ our Lord.
Amen.

Ecclesiastes

For everything there is a season, and a time for every matter under heaven.

<small>ECCLESIASTES 3:1</small>

Opening Prayer

Good teacher,
you give meaning to all things.
You bless us with your gifts.
You strengthen us with your judgment.
Guide us to see the fleeting nature of life.
Help us to hold on to you.
Show us the beauty of life.
Bless us with your grace.
Through Christ our Lord.
Amen.

Basic Message

Life is fluid and fleeting. Our only stability is God. Everything is a gift.

Introductory Overview

The Book of Ecclesiastes is an extended sermon or instruction on the passing nature of life. It calls us to see everything as a gift from God. It warns us not to rely on the things of this world.

Basic Outline

The Book of Ecclesiastes consists of three main parts:

- Chapters 1–4:3: Qoheleth's view of the world.
- Chapters 4:4—9:16: The experiences of wise men.
- Chapters 9:17—12: Counsel to those seeking wisdom.

Application to Our Lives

In Ecclesiastes 3, we are reminded that everything in life has a season. There is a time to live and a time to die, a time for peace and a time for war, a time to plant and a time to harvest. In essence, we have to watch what we do and when. We have to be attentive to the wisdom of God to know the timing and order of things.

As we watch the movements of life, we realize how fluid and fleeting life is. Consequently, we begin to view everything as a gift. If something comes, thanks be to God. If it doesn't come, thanks be to God. Our senses of satisfaction and of fulfillment do not rely on the unstable things of this world. They are anchored in God. We rely on God and his goodness to us.

Learning to rely on God is an important life lesson. We can quickly fall into entitlement, self-pity, anger, and bitterness when things don't go our way or when they play out in ways different from what we wanted or thought we deserved. Such an approach to life is a sure path to agony, misery, and anguish. But this is not how God wants his children to live. Ecclesiastes teaches us to accept what comes and to let go of the things that don't. We are encouraged to see God's care for us and to approach everything as a gift. Such a way of life gives freedom, peace, and joy. This is how we are called to live.

Basic Points

Author: The Jewish and Christian traditions attribute the Book of Ecclesiastes to King Solomon, although several editors worked on the book.

Placement: Ecclesiastes is the twenty-fifth book of the Old Testament. It is part of the wisdom books of the Bible. Ecclesiastes is a supplemental book of the principal narrative books of the Bible.

Keywords:

- *Qoheleth*: The Hebrew word for "teacher" or "preacher." The author of Ecclesiastes gives great deference to "the teacher," who gives the main portion of the book's instruction.
- *Hevel*: The Hebrew word for "vapor" or "smoke." It is used in Ecclesiastes to describe the temporary nature of all created things. It serves as a reminder that nothing is stable or lasting in this life.

Getting Started

The Book of Ecclesiastes is a sustained sermon or instruction consisting of twelve chapters. The goal is to eventually read the book in its entirety. In the meantime, however, here are three selections that can get us started. Each selection shows us the depth and wisdom of Ecclesiastes: a reminder of the importance of friendship (4:9–12); the description of the mystery of God's ways (8:10–17); and the nature of youth and old age (11:7–12:8).

Concluding Prayer

Father of time and space,
you are the beginning and end of all things.
Without you, nothing has value,

nothing has merit.
Bless us with your wisdom.
Show us your goodness.
Grant us your strength.
Through Christ our Lord.
Amen.

Song of Solomon

Set me as a seal upon your heart,
*   as a seal upon your arm;*
for love is strong as death,
*   jealousy is cruel as the grave.*
Its flashes are flashes of fire,
*   a most vehement flame.*

SONG OF SOLOMON 8:6

Opening Prayer
All-loving God,
Father of affection,
source of all goodness,
you call to us. You search for us.
Soften our hearts.
Help us to find you. Help us to trust you.
Embrace us. Console us.
Grant us your fellowship.
Through Christ our Lord.
Amen.

Basic Message
God passionately loves his people. Love is more powerful and stronger than sorrow and death.

Introductory Overview
The Song of Solomon is an extended love poem describing the

desire and affection between two lovers. The poem serves as an allegory of the divine love for humanity. It has a fluctuating rhythm and is filled with symbolic and figurative language.

Basic Outline
The Song of Solomon consists of three main parts:

- Chapters 1–3:5: The courtship.
- Chapters 3:6—5:1: The wedding.
- Chapters 5:2—8:14: Marital love.

Application to Our Lives
In Song of Solomon 8:5–14, the passionate and euphoric love expressed throughout the poem begins to mature. It deepens as we are told of the seal upon the lovers' hearts and arms. We are told that love is stronger than death. Love gives life as a child is announced. Love cannot be enslaved. It cannot be bought by money or controlled by power. It is a garden freely held by the one who loves.

In our lives, we have to allow the first attractions of love to mature. It's easy to enjoy someone's company solely because of that person's physical attraction, intellect, sense of humor, personality, or some other trait that pleases us. But if we truly want to love, we have to allow such initial attraction to deepen. We have to see the other person in the fullness of who he or she is and not just as a superficial someone we enjoy. Our love must honor the other person. It must become sacrificial, always seeking the good of the beloved. It must give life to others and not merely pleasure to ourselves. Love is a strong power of our soul. It can lead us to self-absorption or self-sacrifice, to great evil or glorious virtue. The decision is ours, and it begins with our reaction to initial attraction.

Basic Points
Author: The Jewish and Christian traditions attribute the Song of

Solomon to King Solomon, although several editors worked on the book.

Placement: The Song of Solomon is the twenty-sixth book of the Old Testament. It is part of what are called the wisdom books of the Bible. The Song of Solomon is a supplemental book of the principal narrative books of the Bible.

Keywords:

- Allegory: A story or poem that contains an interior moral message or lesson.
- Passionate attraction or desire: The initial movement of love. Such an attraction either dies out or matures into a deeper love.

Getting Started

The Song of Solomon is a love poem of eight chapters. As a poem, it has an internal fluidity and is best read in its entirety. In the meantime, however, here are two selections that can get us started. Each selection shows us the depth and wisdom of the Song of Solomon: the springtime rhapsody (2:8–17) and the beauty of the bride (chapter 4).

Concluding Prayer

Eternal Father,
you are the love that binds all things.
You care for each of us.
Show us your kindness.
Help us to know your goodness.
Bless us. Stay close to us.
Through Christ our Lord.
Amen.

Wisdom

*Again, one preparing to sail and about
to voyage over raging waves
calls upon a piece of wood more fragile
than the ship which carries him.*

WISDOM 14:1

Opening Prayer
Ever-living God,
Wisdom on High,
teach us your ways.
Show us the path of righteousness.
Give us your strength.
Bless us with your grace.
Through Christ our Lord.
Amen.

Basic Message
Wisdom is the pursuit of righteousness. God rewards the righteous with eternal life.

Introductory Overview
The Book of Wisdom — or the Wisdom of Solomon — is a collection of sayings, maxims, and teachings on eternal life, the nature of wisdom, its place in salvation history, and the way for us to find wisdom in our lives.

Basic Outline

The Book of Wisdom consists of three main parts:

- Chapters 1–5: Meditation on immortality.
- Chapters 6–9: Wisdom and its blessings.
- Chapters 10–19: Wisdom in the course of salvation history.

Application to Our Lives

In Wisdom 14, we hear about idolatry. The section reminds us how futile and hurtful idolatry can be. As human beings, we are made by and for God. Whenever we worship something or someone other than God, we restrict — or prevent — the blessings God wants to give us. In addition, our souls, which need God, cannot receive the spiritual sustenance they need.

Idols are not only wooden statues or marble images. An idol can be any created thing or person. It can be money, sexual pleasure, desire for stability, social acceptance, a beloved person, or any such thing. We have to be attentive to the movements of our hearts. We must order our attractions and desires and refocus them according to divine wisdom and the moral teachings that flow from it.

In our lives, we have to identify what gives us hope, where we seek consolation, and what provides us with peace and stability. It's very easy for our fallen hearts to trick themselves and begin to worship something other than the one, true God. We need to nourish a healthy self-suspicion and regularly do a good examination of conscience so that we can recognize and root out idolatry. Our hearts belong to God. Only he deserves our worship. Only in him can we find hope, consolation, peace, and stability.

Basic Points

Author: The Jewish and Christian traditions attribute the Book of Wisdom to King Solomon, although several editors worked on the book.

Placement: Wisdom is the twenty-seventh book of the Old Testament. It is part of what are called the wisdom books of the Bible. Wisdom is a supplemental book of the principal narrative books of the Bible. Wisdom is also one of the deuterocanonical books. (See Appendix B.)

Keywords:

- Eternal life: The sharing in God's glory for eternity. The reality of eternal life was slowly revealed by God to his people. It was fully revealed in the resurrection of Jesus Christ.
- Idolatry: The false worship of something or someone other than God. Our souls were created for the adoration of God alone. Idolatry, therefore, causes a disorder in our souls.

Getting Started

The Book of Wisdom is a collection of teachings, sayings, and maxims that consist of nineteen chapters. As such, it is an easy book to read in small portions. The goal, however, is to eventually read the book in its entirety. In the meantime, here are three selections that can get us started. Each selection shows us the depth and wisdom of Wisdom: the blindness of the wicked (2:21–24); the triumph of the righteous (4:16–19); and Solomon's prayer for wisdom (chapter 9).

Concluding Prayer
Eternal Father,
Lord of all things,
Source of all that exists,
hear our cry.
Help us to know your ways.
Show us the path of wisdom.
Enlighten our minds.
Strengthen our wills.
Show us your glory.
Through Christ our Lord.
Amen.

Sirach

Then the Creator of all things gave me a commandment,
and the one who created me assigned a place for my tent.
And he said, "Make your dwelling in Jacob,
and in Israel receive your inheritance."

SIRACH 24:8

Opening Prayer
Eternal Father,
Wonderful Counselor,
show us your face.
Help us to know your wisdom.
Bless us with your grace.
Show us your way.
Through Christ our Lord.
Amen.

Basic Message
Wisdom is found in reverence for God and obedience to his teachings.

Introductory Overview
The Book of Sirach is a collection of brief essays, hymns, and psalms that explain aspects of how to seek wisdom through a virtuous and holy life, according to the teachings of God.

Basic Outline
The Book of Sirach consists of three main parts, marked by a hymn in the middle of the book:

- Chapters 1–23: Wisdom and some practical ways of living by its teachings.
- Chapter 24: A hymn to wisdom.
- Chapters 25–51: More practical ways of living wisdom and the heroes of this way of life.

Application to Our Lives
In Sirach 24, we hear a beautiful hymn to divine wisdom. The song resonates with the praise and glory of God. In the midst of the hymn, wisdom tells us that, while she was created and given to all humanity, she was told by God to make her dwelling with Jacob and to make Israel her inheritance.

This account is significant since it teaches us that, while wisdom can be found in many places within human knowledge, wisdom dwells uniquely and powerfully in the teachings of God. Such divine teachings have been entrusted to and held by God's people.

In our lives, we should seek wisdom in all that we do. We should explore all the different fields of human knowledge with a vibrant curiosity and a willingness to learn. In this search, however, we are reminded that divine wisdom is higher than human knowledge. And so we must be vigorous in our study of divine wisdom and seek its help and guidance above all other things. In the teachings of God, we are given a bright lamp to guide our feet.

Basic Points
Author: The Jewish and Christian traditions attribute the Book of Sirach to the Jewish scribe Jesus Ben (son of) Sirach of Jerusalem, although several editors worked on the book.

Placement: Sirach is the twenty-eighth book of the Old Testament. It is part of what are called the wisdom books of the Bible. Sirach is a supplemental book of the principal narrative books of the Bible. Sirach is also one of the deuterocanonical books. (See Appendix B.)

Keywords:

- Ecclesiasticus: The term literally means "book of the Church." It is a popular second name of the Book of Sirach, since the book is used so regularly in the liturgy and teachings of the Church.

Getting Started

The Book of Sirach is a collection of brief essays, hymns, and psalms to the praise of wisdom. It consists of fifty-one chapters. As such, it is an easy book to read in small portions. The goal, however, is to eventually read the book in its entirety. In the meantime, here are three selections that can get us started. Each selection shows us the depth and wisdom of Sirach: wisdom on friendship (6:5–17); the responsible use of wealth (14:3–19); and caution in taking advice (37:7–15).

Concluding Prayer

Everlasting Father,
Ancient of Days,
Beginning and End of all things,
hear our cry.
Give us your wisdom.
Guide us with your Spirit.
Show us the path of righteousness.
Grant us your blessings.
Through Christ our Lord.
Amen.

Prophetic Books

Isaiah	Obadiah
Jeremiah	Jonah
Lamentations	Micah
Baruch*	Nahum
Ezekiel	Habakkuk
Daniel	Zephaniah
Hosea	Haggai
Joel	Zechariah
Amos	Malachi

---

*Deuterocanonical book. (See Appendix B.)

Isaiah

But he was wounded for our transgressions,
he was bruised for our iniquities;
upon him was the chastisement that made us whole,
and with his stripes we are healed.

Isaiah 53:5

Opening Prayer
Lord God,
giver of judgment and hope,
we turn to you.
We hope in you.
Help us in our distress.
Show us your mercy.
Renew our hearts.
Through Christ our Lord.
Amen.

Basic Message
God is holy. He will judge evil and discipline his people. Even as
he disciplines us, he blesses us with hope and seeks our holiness.

Introductory Overview
The Book of Isaiah is a collection of numerous exhortations,
prophecies, and promises of hope that point God's people to
the long-awaited Anointed Savior and a new creation in him. It
spans from the overthrow of the northern kingdom to the return

from the Babylonian Exile after the fall of the southern kingdom.

Basic Outline

The Book of Isaiah consists of two main parts divided by the Babylonian Exile:

- Chapters 1–39: A collection of prophecies and exhortations of judgment against the idolatry and evil actions of God's people.
- Chapters 40–66: A collection of prophecies and exhortations of hope that promises God's people a time of restoration and universal salvation in the Anointed Savior.

Application to Our Lives

In Isaiah 52:13–53:12, we have the "Song of the Suffering Servant," the last of the prophet's four "servant songs." In general, Isaiah's servant songs are a beautiful description of the long-awaited Anointed Savior. They provide some of the clearest biblical explanations of the mission of the Anointed Savior, whom Isaiah simply calls "the servant."

In the fourth song, we see that the Anointed Messiah will suffer. He will be rejected, despised, and beaten. And yet his sufferings will be the source of our healing. The sufferings he will undergo have a redemptive power.

In our lives, we have sufferings, sorrows, heartaches, losses, disappointments, and moments of confusion or bewilderment. In looking at the sufferings of God's servant — which are fulfilled in the passion, death, and resurrection of Jesus Christ — we have great hope. We can unite our sufferings with the sufferings of the servant, the Lord Jesus, and offer them to the Father. Our sorrows will not be removed, but in offering up our sufferings to the Father, they can become redemptive in Jesus Christ.

Darkness does not have to have the last word. Our sufferings can have redemptive power for ourselves, our loved ones, the whole Church, and all humanity. We see this in the saving work of Jesus Christ. In him, we can also see it in our own sufferings.

Basic Points

Author: The Jewish and Christian traditions attribute the Book of Isaiah to Isaiah and his later group of prophetic disciples.

Placement: Isaiah is the twenty-ninth book of the Old Testament. It is part of what are called the prophetic books of the Bible. Isaiah is a supplemental book of the principal narrative books of the Bible.

Keywords:

- Fifth Gospel: The term used in Christian tradition to describe the Book of Isaiah, since the book contains so many prophecies and descriptions of the Anointed Savior. There are only four Gospel Books in the New Testament. The expression *Fifth Gospel*, therefore, shows how significant Isaiah is in understanding Jesus Christ.
- Holy seed: The expression used in Isaiah to describe the people who were faithful to God's covenant in times of massive infidelity. The term *seed* indicates that God would grow — bring forth — something glorious from darker times.

Getting Started

The Book of Isaiah is a collection of numerous exhortations, prophecies, and promises of hope, which point to the Anointed Savior and a new creation in him. It consists of sixty-six chapters. The goal is to read the book in its entirety. In the meantime, however, here are three selections that can get us started. Each selection shows us the depth and wisdom of Isaiah: Isaiah's call to be a prophet (chapter 6); Hezekiah's fall to pride (chapter 39); and the prayer of repentance offered by God's people (63:15—64:12).

Concluding Prayer
All-holy God,
Judge of the living and the dead,
Hope of all people,
come to our aid!
Hear our prayers.
Turn to us.
Show us your mercy.
Grant us your grace.
Renew the face of the earth.
Through Christ our Lord.
Amen.

Jeremiah

Then the word of the LORD came to me: "O house of
Israel, can I not do with you as this potter has done?
says the LORD. Behold, like the clay in the potter's
hand, so are you in my hand, O house of Israel."

JEREMIAH 18:5–6

Opening Prayer
Eternal Father,
you form and discipline your people.
Hear us. Save us from evil.
Correct our faults.
Guide us along your path.
Bless us with your grace.
Show us your glory.
Through Christ our Lord.
Amen.

Basic Message
God is holy. He disciplines his people in order to purify them
and make them holy. Rebellion against God has destructive consequences for people and nations.

Introductory Overview
The Book of Jeremiah is a collection of numerous sermons, poems, and essays by the prophet, relating to God's call to be holy,
the consequences of sin, God's discipline of his people, and the

promises and growing hope for the Anointed Savior. It spans from the end of the southern kingdom to the return from the Babylonian Exile.

Basic Outline

The Book of Jeremiah consists of two main parts divided by the Babylonian Exile:

- Chapters 1–24: The call to holiness and the warnings of God's discipline.
- Chapter 25: God's disciplining his people through Babylon, and the fall of Jerusalem and the exile of God's people.
- Chapters 26–52: The attacks of Babylon on Israel and the nations, and God's humbling of Babylon.

Application to Our Lives

In Jeremiah 18:1–11, we hear the story of God's telling the prophet to go to the potter's house. Once there, God uses the potter's shifting and forming of clay as a teaching tool to explain what he desires to do with each of us. God wants to mold and shape us. He wants us to recognize our dignity and allow him to sculpt and configure us to him and his holiness. But we have to let him work. If we do not, then God will bring discipline upon us.

We have many ideas and plans for our lives. Oftentimes things don't go the way we want, and we can let those disappointments compromise our trust in God. We begin to lose our focus, seeking to mold and shape God to fit into our wants and our plans, rather than allowing him to sculpt and design us. In these moments, God will not allow himself or his fatherly care to be hijacked. He will respond with discipline and allow us to endure the consequences of our rebellion. Rather than living through a spiritual Babylonian exile, we need to draw close to

God, seek his wisdom, obey his commands, and stay faithful to him and his covenant. In this way, we allow God to draw close to us, bless us, and give us his grace.

Basic Points

Author: The Jewish and Christian traditions attribute the Book of Jeremiah to the prophet Jeremiah and his scribe, Baruch.

Placement: Jeremiah is the thirtieth book of the Old Testament. It is part of what are called the prophetic books of the Bible. Jeremiah is a supplemental book of the principal narrative books of the Bible.

Keywords:

- Babylonian Exile: The exile of God's people from the Promised Land of their forefathers. The exile came after the destruction of Jerusalem and the Temple of Solomon. The exile lasted seventy years and was a severe discipline by God upon his people for their infidelities to his covenant.
- Destruction of the Temple and the loss of the Ark of the Covenant: God's severest discipline of his people in the Old Testament. The destruction of the Temple and the loss of the Ark indicated the loss of God's Spirit among his people. It led to a profound sense of bewilderment and spiritual displacement among God's people.

Getting Started

The Book of Jeremiah is a collection of numerous sermons, poems, and essays that point to the Anointed Savior and a new kingdom in him. It consists of fifty-two chapters. The goal is to read the book in its entirety. In the meantime, however, here are three selections that can get us started. Each selection shows us the depth and wisdom of Jeremiah: Jeremiah's call as a prophet (1:4–10); Jeremiah's infamous "temple sermon" (chapter 7); and Jeremiah's words of hope for the future (chapters 30–33).

Concluding Prayer

God of justice and grace,
look upon us in our need.
Hear our cry.
Help us to draw close to you.
Inspire us. Strengthen us.
Keep us faithful to your teachings.
Through Christ our Lord.
Amen.

Lamentations

How lonely sits the city
  that was full of people!
How like a widow has she become,
  she that was great among the nations!
She that was a princess among the cities
  has become a vassal.

LAMENTATIONS 1:1

Opening Prayer
Heavenly Father,
Consolation of your people,
Hope of the nations,
we turn to you.
We repent.
We grieve our sins.
We beg your mercy.
We seek your fellowship.
Come to us.
Show us your glory.
Through Christ our Lord.
Amen.

Basic Message
God hears the cries of his people as they grieve their sin and its
consequences.

Introductory Overview

The Book of Lamentations is a collection of five psalms expressing the grief of God's people over the siege and fall of Jerusalem. The book is a memorial to the displacement and perplexity of God's people over the destruction of Jerusalem and the loss of the Promised Land.

Basic Outline

The Book of Lamentations consists of five songs or psalms. Each song is its own chapter.

- Chapter 1: The description of Jerusalem as a widow.
- Chapter 2: The fall of Jerusalem as an expression of God's wrath.
- Chapter 3: The suffering of God's people as depicted in one man's grief.
- Chapter 4: A parallel of life before and after the siege of Jerusalem.
- Chapter 5: A plea for mercy.

Application to Our Lives

In Lamentations 1, we hear of daughter Zion, a personification of Jerusalem after her siege and destruction by Babylon. Daughter Zion is a widow and is grieving the loss of God and the blessings he bestowed upon her. She feels completely lost and bewildered. And yet she thanks God for the discipline he has given to her. She further petitions him to humble others who have offended him.

In our lives, correction is difficult to accept. Whether discipline is offered by a family member, an employer, a neighbor, or some other person, we tend to resist it. We might become defensive. We might blame others, deflect and deny, or refuse to accept responsibility or admit accountability. We might argue about the demeanor or tone of the one correcting us. When this happens, we can miss opportunities to improve ourselves and our abilities. Daughter Zion accepted her plight because she knew she was guilty. In accepting her responsibility, she allowed God to raise her up and bestow new blessings upon her. In our lives, we have to do the same when we are disciplined. We must humbly accept such correction and seek to become better people.

Basic Points

Author: The Jewish and Christian traditions attribute the Book of Lamentations to Baruch, the scribe of the prophet Jeremiah.

Placement: Lamentations is the thirty-first book of the Old Testament. It is part of what are called the prophetic books of the Bible. Lamentations is a supplemental book of the principal narrative books of the Bible.

Keywords:

- Daughter Zion: The popular term used to personify Jerusalem, whom the prophet presents as a widow, having suffered the loss of intimacy with her divine spouse. And yet God hears her cry and comes to her aid.
- God's wrath: The biblical term for God's justice. It should not be confused with unrestrained anger or vengeance but is rather a disciplined exercise of justice that addresses wrongdoing and seeks reform and reconciliation.

Getting Started

The Book of Lamentations is a collection of five psalms that express the heartbreak of God's people over the fall of Jerusalem. It consists of five chapters. As such, it's an easy read in one sitting. In the meantime, however, it's worth reading these two selections: the hope of God's people as they suffer God's discipline (3:19–24) and the plea for mercy (chapter 5).

Concluding Prayer
Almighty and ever-living God,
you are the one who disciplines;
you are the one who heals.
Correct our faults.
Forgive our transgressions.
Show us your mercy.
Through Christ our Lord.
Amen.

Baruch

We did not heed the voice of the Lord our God in all the words of the prophets whom he sent to us.

BARUCH 1:21

Opening Prayer
All-holy God,
you create and sustain all things.
You cast down only to build back up.
You discipline in order to bless.
Hear our cry.
Forgive our sins.
Heal us. Restore us.
Bless us with your mercy.
Show us your glory.
Through Christ our Lord.
Amen.

Basic Message
God does not forget us, even when he disciplines us because of our sinfulness.

Introductory Overview
The Book of Baruch is a collection of prayers, prophecies, psalms, and letters. The book expresses the spiritual state of God's people who are in exile in Babylon away from their home in Jerusalem in the Promised Land.

Basic Outline

The Book of Baruch consists of six chapters:

- Chapter 1: Confession of sins.
- Chapter 2: Prayer of petition.
- Chapter 3: Petition and the praise of wisdom in the law of Moses.
- Chapter 4: Psalm of hope and encouragement for Jerusalem.
- Chapter 5: Continued psalm of hope and encouragement.
- Chapter 6: Denunciation of idolatry.

Application to Our Lives

In Baruch 1:15–21, the people in exile are repenting of their sins and expressing sorrow and heartache over the loss of Jerusalem. They are away from home and feeling an immense spiritual homesickness. Their dejection is magnified because they realize they have caused their own plight. They are the only ones to blame. God sent them prophets and warnings, exhortations and admonitions, and they did not listen to wisdom. They rejected any correction or help.

In our lives, God sends us friends, loved ones, mentors, and teachers. Many of these people fulfill a contemporary role much like the one that the prophets of old fulfilled in Jerusalem. In our day, we have to humble ourselves and listen to the wisdom that is given to us. We have to remind ourselves that no human being has all the answers, and no one knows everything. It's good to ask for help and receive instruction or mentoring. God continues to work among his people. The ones who want to help us have been sent to us. God is trying to give us wisdom. We must have open ears and open hearts so that we can learn everything that God is trying to teach us.

Basic Points

Author: The Jewish and Christian traditions attribute the Book of Baruch to Baruch, the scribe of the prophet Jeremiah.

Placement: Baruch is the thirty-second book of the Old Testament. It is part of what are called the prophetic books of the Bible. Baruch is a supplemental book of the principal narrative books of the Bible. Baruch is also one of the deuterocanonical books. (See Appendix B.)

Keywords:

- Diaspora: The term for all the lands outside the Promised Land of God's people. When God's people were dispersed from the Promised Land, they were sent into the diaspora, i.e., other lands beyond their borders.
- Hope: A confident trust in God and the opportunity to be with him. It is not a trust in human power or talents or in any human state of affairs. Hope is trust in God and a longing to be with him.

Getting Started

The Book of Baruch is a collection of prayers, prophecies, psalms, and letters. They each express the heartbreak of God's people as they are dispersed among the nations and away from Jerusalem and the Promised Land of their forefathers. The book consists of six chapters. As such, it's an easy read in one sitting. In the meantime, however, it's worth reading about God's encouragement to his exiled people (4:5–29) and the complete helplessness of graven idols (6:8–40).

Concluding Prayer
Eternal God,
you are always with your people.
Even when you feel far away from us,
you are always close.
Even when you discipline us,
you are there to console and encourage.
Renew us, Lord.
Bless us. Strengthen us.
Forgive our transgressions.
Show us your glory.
Through Christ our Lord.
Amen.

Ezekiel

*Thus says the Lord GOD to these bones: Behold, I
will cause breath to enter you, and you shall live.*

EZEKIEL 37:5

Opening Prayer

O God,
glorious and majestic,
we praise you!
You alone are holy.
You alone are the life of your people.
Come to us.
Renew our hearts.
Send us your Spirit.
We adore you. We follow you.
Show us your glory!
Through Christ our Lord.
Amen.

Basic Message

God is all-holy and majestic beyond words. We are not able to
give God everything he deserves, so he will give us new hearts to
love and serve him.

Introductory Overview

The Book of Ezekiel is a collection of the prophet's visions, teachings, and prophecies. Since Ezekiel was a priest, the book gives

extensive attention to the worship of God, the Temple, and the liturgies of God's people. The book emphasizes that true worship requires a new heart with an internal conversion to God.

Basic Outline
The Book of Ezekiel consists of four main parts:

- Chapters 1–11: Accusations against the idolatry and covenant violations of God's people.
- Chapters 12–32: God's judgment on his people and the nations of the world.
- Chapter 33: The fall of Jerusalem.
- Chapters 34–48: A future hope for God's people, for all the nations of the world, and for all creation.

Application to Our Lives
In Ezekiel 37:1–14, God gives the prophet a tour of a valley filled with bones, and Ezekiel observes that the bones look very dry. God asks the prophet whether the bones could live. When Ezekiel replies, "O Lord GOD, you know" (37:3), God orders him to prophesy that the bones would come back to life. Ezekiel obeys, and, true to God's word, the bones take on muscles and flesh and come back to life!

After such a powerful miracle, God tells Ezekiel to instruct his people that, as he brought the bones back to life so he could give them new life, return them to the Promised Land from which they had been exiled, and restore his covenant, which they had broken and which appeared dead.

In our lives, there can be times when everything seems dark, and death surrounds us. We can grieve, struggle with melancholy, wrestle with our weakness, and feel as if there is no hope. In such moments, God asks us, as he did Ezekiel: Do you think these bones can live? Do you think this darkness is the end? And just as God did in the valley, so he can do in our lives. He can show us the way out of darkness, remind us we're not alone, and give us strength to slowly put things back together and live in his abundant grace. This powerful work was done in the life of the prophet Ezekiel. It can be done in our lives, if we let it.

Basic Points

Author: The Jewish and Christian traditions attribute the Book of Ezekiel to the prophet Ezekiel, although other writers and editors worked on the book.

Placement: Ezekiel is the thirty-third book of the Old Testament. It is part of what are called the prophetic books of the Bible. Ezekiel is a supplemental book of the principal narrative books of the Bible.

Keywords:

- Four living creatures: The four angelic beings who surround the presence of God. They are often described as appearing as a man, a lion, an ox, and an eagle.
- Sign acts: The method used by the prophets to get people's attention and communicate divine wisdom. It was a dramatic combination of show-and-tell, charades, symbolic theatrics, and shock-jock tactics.

Getting Started

The Book of Ezekiel is a collection of the prophet's visions, teachings, and prophecies. While the eventual goal is to read all forty-eight chapters of the Book of Ezekiel, here are three selections that can get us started. Each selection shows us the depth and wisdom of Ezekiel: the prophet's call by God (chapter 2); God's promise of blessings and a new heart to his people (36:16–38); and the living river that flows to all the nations (47:1–12).

Concluding Prayer

Heavenly Father,
you are all-holy
and worthy of all our devotion.
Convert our hearts.
Help us to love you.
Give us your grace.
Turn our hearts to you.
Bless us. Strengthen us.
Show us your glory.
Through Christ our Lord.
Amen.

Daniel

He was driven from among men, and ate grass like an ox, and his body was wet with the dew of heaven till his hair grew as long as eagles' feathers, and his nails were like birds' claws.

DANIEL 4:33B

Opening Prayer
O God,
Ancient of Days,
glorious and majestic,
you are all-holy!
Hear our prayers.
Do not turn your face from us.
Send us your Spirit.
Show us your glory!
Through Christ our Lord.
Amen.

Basic Message
God is the Lord of all history. He works through the empires and governments of humanity to show forth his presence and his glory.

Introductory Overview
The Book of Daniel is a collection of the stories, visions, and prophecies of the prophet Daniel. The collection shows God's

actions in various empires and governments. It displays God's faithfulness and kindness to those who love him and his discipline to those who disobey and reject him.

Basic Outline

The Book of Daniel consists of three main parts:

- Chapters 1–6: Stories of Daniel and his friends.
- Chapters 7–12: The visions of Daniel and the future glory of God's people.
- Chapters 13–14: Heroic stories of Daniel.

Application to Our Lives

In Daniel 4, King Nebuchadnezzar is described as a powerful king filled with a prideful spirit. God warns the king to humble himself before him. Nebuchadnezzar refuses.

As a consequence, King Nebuchadnezzar takes on the appearance of a monstrous beast, a hybrid of wild animals. The king sees his dilemma, repents, and humbles himself before God. In response, the Lord heals him physically and mentally and restores him to his throne.

When we allow pride and arrogance to fill our hearts, we can give a wide-open permission to cruelty, unkindness, slander, dismissiveness, and condescension. We become less human. At our worst, we can act like a hybrid of wild animals, rather than children of God. Our sin diminishes our goodness and identity in the Lord. By repenting and humbling ourselves before God, we become more what and who God has called us to be. As we fight against sin and seek virtue in our lives, we fulfill our vocation as God's children.

Basic Points

Author: The Jewish and Christian traditions attribute the Book of Daniel to the prophet Daniel, although other writers and editors worked on the book.

Placement: Daniel is the thirty-fourth book of the Old Testament. It is part of what are called the prophetic books of the Bible. Daniel is a supplemental book of the principal narrative books of the Bible.

Keywords:

- Son of man: The term used in the Book of Daniel to describe the king of the covenant who is defeated by evil but is made victorious by God. Later in salvation history, Jesus Christ will use this title for himself.
- Writing on the wall: In the Book of Daniel, the miraculous writing by human fingers warning King Belshazzar of his pride and its consequences. The king refused the warning and was assassinated. This biblical wonder has become a popular metaphor to describe an obvious or easily discernible state of affairs.

Getting Started

The Book of Daniel is a collection of the stories, visions, and prophecies of Daniel. While the eventual goal is to read all fourteen chapters of the Book of Daniel, here are three selections that can get us started. Each selection shows us the depth and wisdom of Daniel: the young men in the fiery furnace (3:19–97); Daniel in the lion's den (chapter 6); and the righteous woman Susanna (chapter 13).

Concluding Prayer
Eternal God,
Lord of history,
Beginning and End of all things,
come to our aid.
Convert us. Strengthen us.
Fortify our hearts.
Keep us faithful to you.
We praise you. We adore you.
Through Christ our Lord.
Amen.

Hosea

*When the Lord first spoke through Hosea,
the Lord said to Hosea, "Go, take to yourself a wife
of harlotry and have children of harlotry, for the land
commits great harlotry by forsaking the Lord."*

Hosea 1:2

Opening Prayer
O God,
Husband of Israel,
faithful Spouse of your people,
we repent of our sins.
We turn away from our idolatry.
We turn to you. We seek your face.
We love you. We adore you.
Call us to yourself.
Show us your love.
Protect us.
Keep us faithful to you.
Show us your glory!
Through Christ our Lord.
Amen.

Basic Message
God loves us and is faithful to us, even when we do not love and
stay faithful to him and his covenant.

Introductory Overview

The Book of Hosea is the story of the prophet Hosea's broken marriage, which serves as a prophetic symbol of the broken covenant between God and his people.

Basic Outline

The Book of Hosea consists of three main parts:

- Chapters 1–3: The broken marriage of Hosea and Gomer.
- Chapters 4–13: Judgment against God's people because of their infidelities.
- Chapter 14: God's reconciliation with his people.

Application to Our Lives

In Hosea 1, God calls on Hosea to marry a known prostitute. Hosea obeys and enters into a marriage covenant with Gomer. The couple has three children. Sadly, Gomer is unfaithful and repeatedly commits adultery. Hosea is humiliated as he has to go and retrieve his wife from the home of her lover. God commands his prophet to live this life so that Gomer would know of Hosea's true love for her (3:1–3).

The marriage also serves as a prophetic symbol for God's people. As Gomer is unfaithful to Hosea, so God's people have been unfaithful to him. God is in a covenant — a spiritual marriage — with his people, and yet they gravely betray him. They turn to false gods and other forms of idolatry. They violate God's moral law and mock him among the nations. And yet God is faithful. He loves his people. He will not abandon them. Rather, he pursues them and seeks them out. He desires to restore them as his beloved.

In our lives, we need to realize the weight and beauty of marriage. God created marriage. It is a covenant, a solemn oath in which two become one. It is a reflection of the union God has with his people, so it touches the very heart of God. Marriage is sacred. It merits the respect of society and the esteem of those who are called to it. We look to Hosea to see this witness. He loved Gomer and showed her — in spite of her infidelities — how much he loved her and how holy marriage is. Spouses are given the command to love and honor each other. They are to be faithful and mutually serve each other with a selfless and kind spirit. Marriage is not an easy way of life, but it is a good and holy one. It points to God himself and gives a witness to his love and faithfulness.

Basic Points

Author: The Jewish and Christian traditions attribute the Book of Hosea to the prophet Hosea, although other writers and editors worked on the book.

Placement: Hosea is the thirty-fifth book of the Old Testament. It is part of what are called the prophetic books of the Bible. Hosea is a supplemental book of the principal narrative books of the Bible.

Keywords:

- Husband: The image used for God by the prophet Hosea. It is a popular image among the prophets of the north. It expresses God's love and faithfulness for his people.
- Ephraim: The mega tribe that was created by the merging of ten of the twelve tribes of God's people. Ephraim held the north and became another name for the northern kingdom, which was also called Israel, after the division of David's kingdom.

Getting Started

The Book of Hosea is the story of the life, prophecies, and teachings of the prophet Hosea. While the eventual goal is to read all fourteen chapters of the Book of Hosea, here are three selections that can get us started. Each selection shows us the depth and wisdom of Hosea: a call to repentance (6:1–3); the expression of God's tenderness (chapter 11); and the rebellion of God's people (chapters 12–13).

Concluding Prayer

Loving Father,
you teach your people to walk;
you help us when we stumble.
Turn to us.
We repent of our infidelities.
Help us to be faithful.
Convert our hearts.
Show us your tenderness.
Through Christ our Lord.
Amen.

Joel

And the LORD roars from Zion,
and utters his voice from Jerusalem,
and the heavens and the earth shake.
But the LORD is a refuge to his people,
a stronghold to the people of Israel.

JOEL 3:16

Opening Prayer

O God of justice and love,
your day comes upon us.
We repent of our sins.
We seek your protection.
Cast out the locusts of sin.
Convert our hearts.
Call us to yourself.
Protect us.
Show us your glory!
Through Christ our Lord.
Amen.

Basic Message

God will intervene in human affairs to protect and care for us.

Introductory Overview

The Book of Joel is a heavily biblical interpretation of an infestation of locusts that happened in the Promised Land at some point after the return from Babylon. The swarm of locusts is used by the prophet as a lesson about God's discipline and the forthcoming Day of the Lord, in which all the nations will be conquered, and God's people will receive his Spirit.

Basic Outline

The Book of Joel consists of two main parts:

- Chapters 1–2:27: The locust plague and the Day of the Lord.
- Chapters 2:28—3:21: Blessings and judgment in the final Day of the Lord.

Application to Our Lives

Throughout the Book of Joel, the prophet quotes extensively from other parts of the Bible. He quotes Exodus and shows a thorough knowledge of the early events of salvation history. Joel also cites the writings of the prophets Isaiah, Jeremiah, Ezekiel, Amos, Obadiah, Nahum, Zephaniah, and Malachi. The prophet is completely imbued with the word of God. He has studied it, knows it, and applies it to a tragic event in his day.

Joel looks at the sufferings caused by a locust infestation in the land. He places the event within the biblical narrative and applies divine lessons and wisdom to it. Joel is a man of God. He is a man of the word of God. In these ways, Joel is a model for us.

In our lives, we need to read and study the word of God. It is a living word with endless applications. It was given to us for instruction. Knowing God's word allows us to apply its wisdom to the events, sorrows, and confusions of our day. God does not want us to live as orphans; we are his children. He wants to teach us and guide us, especially through his word. He wants to show us his love and care. So we need to strive to encounter and listen to his word. We need to work to read the Bible and apply its instruction to our lives.

Basic Points

Author: The Jewish and Christian traditions attribute the Book of Joel to the prophet Joel, although other writers and editors worked on the book.

Placement: Joel is the thirty-sixth book of the Old Testament. It is part of what are called the prophetic books of the Bible. Joel is a supplemental book of the principal narrative books of the Bible.

Keywords:

- Progressive fulfillment: The completion of a promise in several ways over the course of time. God gives a progressive fulfillment of his promises throughout the Bible. Joel uses this understanding to show how God could fulfill a promise in his day but also fulfill the same promise in the final Day of the Lord.

Getting Started

The Book of Joel is the account of a locust infestation in the Promised Land. The event is placed in a biblical context and is used to describe the final Day of the Lord. The book consists of three relatively short chapters. As such, it is recommended that the book be read in its entirety.

Concluding Prayer

O God of justice,
you are Teacher and Healer of your people.
You discipline us. You lift us up.

Send your Spirit upon us.
Help us to know your will.
Free us from the plagues and sorrows of our day.
Show us your tenderness.
Grant us your grace.
Through Christ our Lord.
Amen.

Amos

Hear this word that the Lord *has spoken against*
you, O sons of Israel, against the whole family
which I brought up out of the land of Egypt:
"You only have I known
  of all the families of the earth;
therefore I will punish you
  for all your iniquities."

Amos 3:1–2

Opening Prayer
O God,
Living Water to your people,
teach us justice.
Instruct us in compassion.
Turn our hearts to those in need.
Help us to love you.
Show us your glory!
Through Christ our Lord.
Amen.

Basic Message
God does not need our lip service or empty worship. He calls us
to love him and to love those in need.

Introductory Overview
The Book of Amos contains some of the strongest prophetic

teaching in the Bible. It recounts the preaching, prophecies, and visions of the prophet Amos in the northern kingdom, especially regarding the idolatrous temple at Bethel. The prophet emphasizes true worship and a love for the poor and those in need.

Basic Outline

The Book of Amos consists of three main parts:

- Chapters 1–2: Judgment on the nations and on Israel.
- Chapters 3–6: The guilt of God's people and their leadership.
- Chapters 7–9: Visions of judgment and a glimmer of hope for the future.

Application to Our Lives

In Amos 3, God brings judgment against his people. Having denounced the wickedness of the nations that surround them, God delivers a message to his people. He reminds them how he chose them above all others. Since they were chosen and given greater blessings, their discipline will be more severe than what the other nations received. In summary, God is teaching us: to whom much is given, much is expected. When the expectation is not met, discipline will follow.

In our lives, we are called to understand and realize all that God has given to us. As such, the Lord has a higher expectation for each of us, his disciples. He has blessed us, giving us his grace so we can give witness to his mercy, justice, kindness, and compassion. We are to live differently from those who do not believe. Our life as God's people has to be different. This challenge can be a great weight for us, but God gives us his strength and power to accomplish his will. If we neglect or falter in this summons, God will discipline us and guide us to greater faithfulness.

Basic Points

Author: The Jewish and Christian traditions attribute the Book of Amos to the prophet Amos, although other writers and redactors worked on the book.

Placement: Amos is the thirty-seventh book of the Old Testament. It is part of what are called the prophetic books of the Bible. Amos is a supplemental book of the principal narrative books of the Bible.

Keywords:

- Bethel: One of the major temples of the northern kingdom. The temple was notorious for its worship of false gods. It was the principal location for Amos's preaching.
- Care of the poor: God commanded justice from his people. Justice is to give both God and other people their due. As such, it means to worship God wholeheartedly and serve generously the poor and others in need. The false gods of the northern kingdom did not call for justice. As idolatry increased, so did neglect of the poor and others in need.

Getting Started

The Book of Amos is the account of the prophet's teachings, prophecies, and visions. The book consists of nine chapters. While the goal is to read the book in its entirety, here are three selections that can get us started. Each selection shows us the depth and wisdom of Amos: the consequences of self-indulgence (chapter 6); God's defense of the poor and others who are vulnerable (8:4–6); and a message of hope for the future (9:11–15).

Concluding Prayer

Father of the poor,
Defender of the weak,
you are a shepherd and guardian of your people.
Turn to us.
We worship you with our whole hearts.
We adore you. We live by your justice.
Show us the ones in need.
Open our hearts. Grant us humility.
Strengthen us to serve.
Through Christ our Lord.
Amen.

Obadiah

But you should not have gloated over the day of
your brother
in the day of his misfortune;
you should not have rejoiced over the people of Judah
in the day of their ruin;
you should not have boasted
in the day of distress.

OBADIAH 12

Opening Prayer

O God,
you know all things.
You bring justice to your people
and judgment upon the nations.
Hear our plea.
Look upon us with compassion.
Guide us along your path.
Teach us your commands.
Show us your glory!
Through Christ our Lord.
Amen.

Basic Message

God blesses the humble and rejects the proud.

Introductory Overview

The Book of Obadiah is the shortest book of the Old Testament. It contains the preaching and prophecies of the prophet Obadiah against the pride of the people of Edom. The Edomites were related to God's people through the twin brothers Jacob and Esau. The Edomites, however, abandoned the true worship of God and caused tension to God's people. They did not help their "brother Jacob" when the Babylonians destroyed Jerusalem and took God's people into exile. In fact, they even assisted the Babylonians in their attack.

Obadiah contains only one chapter, and so citations from Obadiah include only the verses. For example, "Obadiah 12" means Obadiah, chapter 1, verse 12.

Basic Outline

The Book of Obadiah consists of two main parts within a single chapter:

- Verses 1–14: God's promise that prideful Edom will be humbled.
- Verses 15–21: God's judgment upon the nations and the promise of a new Jerusalem.

Application to Our Lives

In Obadiah, verse 12, God admonishes the Edomites, saying they should have humbled themselves and helped his people when the Babylonians attacked them. Instead, the Edomites plundered cities in the Promised Land and attacked refugees who were fleeing after the Babylonians invaded. In general, God denounces such violence. In particular, he disciplines the Edomites because they are related to his people. Through ancient blood lineage, the Edomites are "brothers" to God's people. As such, they are especially held accountable, since brother is expected to help brother.

In our lives, sibling rivalry (even into adulthood) can be a challenge. We can dismiss a difficult sibling, neglect a brother, or refuse to help a sister. We can rationalize such actions and convince ourselves that we are justified. But, the fact is, God is the one who chose that sibling for us. We are family. Perhaps God sent us a troublesome sibling because he knew we could love that sibling in spite of whatever shortcomings he or she might have. God's plan for us is vast and beautiful. It is sorrowful at times, joyful at others. It involves fulfilling our duties, especially to family. The Edomites didn't understand that truth, but hopefully each of us will.

Basic Points
Author: The Jewish and Christian traditions attribute the Book of Obadiah to the prophet Obadiah, although other writers and redactors worked on the book.

Placement: Obadiah is the thirty-eighth book of the Old Testament. It is part of what are called the prophetic books of the Bible. Obadiah is a supplemental book of the principal narrative books of the Bible.

Keywords:

- Jacob and Esau: The grandsons of Abraham and the twin sons of Isaac and Rebekah. The two brothers had a tense relationship. Jacob is renamed Israel (Gn 32:28) and becomes a patriarch of God's people. Esau is renamed Edom (Gn 25:30) and is the father of the Edomites. (See Genesis 25–27.)
- The heights: The reference to where the Edomites lived. The tribe dwelled in the desert mountains east

of the Promised Land. The term is given a double meaning by Obadiah, as a reference to the pride of the Edomites.

Getting Started

The Book of Obadiah provides the prophet's teachings and prophecies to the Edomites. It consists of twenty-one verses in one chapter. Because the book is so short, it's recommended that it be read in one sitting, but here are some passages to help us: a version of the Golden Rule (verse 15) and the triumph of the righteous (verse 21).

Concluding Prayer

Father of the humble,
Guardian of the oppressed,
you bless your people.
You call families together.
You give them their names.
You summon us to love one another.
Strengthen our hearts.
Help us to serve.
Show us your glory.
Through Christ our Lord.
Amen.

Jonah

And he prayed to the LORD and said, "I pray you, LORD,
is not this what I said when I was yet in my country? That
is why I made haste to flee to Tarshish; for I knew that
you are a gracious God and merciful, slow to anger,
and abounding in mercy, and that you repent of evil."

JONAH 4:2

Opening Prayer

O God,
you are compassionate and kind in all your ways.
You love all your children,
even those we struggle with.
Help us to understand your ways.
Teach us to love as you love.
Guide us to forgive as you forgive.
Give us your strength.
Show us your glory!
Through Christ our Lord.
Amen.

Basic Message

God passionately loves and seeks to forgive all people, even our enemies. God hates no one.

Introductory Overview

The Book of Jonah is a satirical work of historical fiction. It is placed in the prophetic books, rather than the historical books, because of its important message. Unlike the other prophetic books, it is more about the life and struggles of a prophet than a collection of his teachings and prophecies. The life of Jonah is a satire of the struggles of God's people. As Jonah struggled with the mercy of God toward the other nations, so God's people asked the same question. The book was written after God's people returned from their exile in Babylon. As they were re-building Jerusalem, they questioned the success and power of their enemies, especially the mercy and benevolence that God showed them. In the life and struggles of Jonah, these questions are answered.

It's important to note the exaggeration that is a part of satire. The exact historical nature of many of the parts of Jonah is not the priority. The focus is the message behind the story. In the case of the Book of Jonah, the emphasis is God's mercy and love for all his people.

Basic Outline

The Book of Jonah consists of four chapters:

- Chapter 1: The call of the prophet and his attempt to escape.
- Chapter 2: Jonah in the belly of a whale and his prayer for deliverance.
- Chapter 3: Jonah's preaching and Nineveh's repentance.
- Chapter 4: Jonah's anger and God's merciful love.

Application to Our Lives

In Jonah 4, the prophet reveals all. He tells God that he fled his prophetic call because he knows how merciful and compassionate the Lord is and, thus, that he would forgive and bless the

Ninevites. He disagrees with God's mercy and does not want to be a part of it. As he explains this to God, he is outside Nineveh, angry that the city has repented and that God — as he had suspected — has forgiven and blessed this enemy nation.

In response, God makes a tree grow up and cover Jonah with shade. The prophet enjoys the shade, but then God sends a worm to kill the tree. The tree dies, and Jonah no longer has shade. The prophet is doubly upset now. God asks Jonah if he is upset about the tree, a trivial thing for which he did not labor, and then asks whether the Lord should not care about the Ninevites, who are human persons, just like Jonah. There is no answer recorded by the prophet, and the question is really for each of us as well. Do we understand how much God loves all his children, even those who have hurt us, or offended us, or who are our enemies?

In our lives, the provocative message of Jonah is very much needed. When we are hurt or offended, or when someone has injured us or our loved ones, we can want vengeance. We want God to "take our side," but God is the Father of all, and so he seeks the good of all. He will reprove the offense of others as much as he reproves our lack of mercy. The prophetic message of Jonah calls us out of the darkness of our hurt, offense, and defensiveness. It invites us to be free. It summons us to experience the mercy of God in a radical way in our own lives. As God is merciful, so we are called to be merciful.

Basic Points

Author: The Jewish and Christian traditions attribute the Book of Jonah to the prophet Jonah, although other writers and editors worked on the book.

Placement: Jonah is the thirty-ninth book of the Old Testament. It is part of what are called the prophetic books of the Bible. Jonah is a supplemental book of the principal narrative books of the Bible.

Keywords:

- Satire: A literary genre that uses humor, irony, or exaggeration to reveal the faults or misunderstandings of others.

- Nineveh: The capital of the Babylonian Empire, known for its indulgence in excessive violence and sexual depravity. The city's name was a synonym for "grave sin."

Getting Started

The Book of Jonah is a fast-paced, highly emotional, and easy-to-read account. It consists of four relatively small chapters. Because the book is so short, it's recommended that it be read in one sitting — in particular, the famous story of Jonah and the whale (chapters 1–2).

Concluding Prayer

Father of all,
you seek the best for your children.
When we lose ourselves and run from you,
come and search for us.
Embrace us, and do not let us go.
Have mercy on us. Blot out our offenses.
Heal us. Teach us your ways.
Help us to be merciful as you are merciful.
Strengthen us to follow you.
Help us to be instruments of your mercy.
Through Christ our Lord.
Amen.

Micah

He has showed you, O man, what is good;
and what does the LORD require of you
but to do justice, and to love kindness,
and to walk humbly with your God?

MICAH 6:8

Opening Prayer

O God of our forefathers,
you remember Jacob and the holy ones;
come to our assistance.
Guide us to do justice.
Strengthen us to love tenderly.
Help us to walk humbly with you.
We praise you. We adore you.
Through Christ our Lord.
Amen.

Basic Message

God will bless us when we repent of our sins. He will allow discipline to come to us if we do not repent.

Introductory Overview

The Book of Micah is a collection of the prophet's teachings, visions, and prophecies. The pattern of Micah's preaching follows an interplay of "threat-promise." The prophet convicts God's people of their sin and calls for repentance. If they repent, God promises his mercy and blessings. Micah's preaching includes a strong condemnation of the wealthy who have taken advantage of the poor, the weak, and the vulnerable.

Basic Outline

The Book of Micah consists of three main parts:

- Chapters 1–2: Punishment upon God's people with the promise of a remnant of believers.
- Chapters 3–5: Punishment upon the leaders of God's people with the promise of a new Jerusalem.
- Chapters 6–7: God's judgment upon his people and the promise of restoration and steadfast love.

Application to Our Lives

In Micah 6, the prophet summarizes what God wants from his people: justice, love, and humility. These three things encapsulate all of God's moral law and teachings.

While the summary is heartfelt and uplifting, the context can sometimes be lost. Micah is not presenting these as maxims of wisdom or words of encouragement. The call to do justice, love tenderly, and walk humbly is given as an admonition. Micah is teaching these because God's people have failed to do them. They were given as judgments convicting God's people of their wrongdoing. God's people should not have followed the sinful path of other nations and peoples. They were not to pursue the road of the unbeliever. God's people, chosen and blessed by him, should distinguish themselves by their justice, love, and humility.

In our lives, the message of Micah can also be a judgment. It convicts us about how we should live. It pushes us to realize the difference we should make in the midst of the human family. We are God's people, called to be a people of justice, love, and humility. These are not the markers of an easy path, but they are the markers of a people consecrated to God and seeking to follow his way. This is our daily invitation to do justice, love tenderly, and walk humbly. This is how we are called to live. This is the witness we are called to give.

Basic Points

Author: The Jewish and Christian traditions attribute the Book of Micah to the prophet Micah, although other writers and editors worked on the book.

Placement: Micah is the fortieth book of the Old Testament. It is part of what are called the prophetic books of the Bible. Micah is a supplemental book of the principal narrative books of the Bible.

Keywords:

- Bethlehem: The prophet Micah is the one who was given the knowledge that the long-awaited Anointed Savior would come from Bethlehem, the hometown of King David (see 5:1–3).

Getting Started

The Book of Micah is a narrative of the prophet's preaching and warnings. It's marked by a back-and-forth movement of threats and promises. As such, it's fast-paced and relatively easy to read. It consists of seven chapters. While the goal is to eventually read the book in its entirety, here are three selections that can get us started. Each selection shows us the depth and wisdom of Micah: God's shepherding of his faithful people (2:12–13); peace and security through obedience to God (4:1–5); and God's steadfast love (7:18–20).

Concluding Prayer
Father love,
Guardian of justice,
Lover of humility,
we come before you.
We have only broken hearts and empty hands.
Show us your mercy and compassion.
Forgive our sins. Heal our brokenness.
Lift us up. Restore us.
Help us to see your beauty.
Bless us with your presence.
Through Christ our Lord.
Amen.

Nahum

Who can stand before his indignation?
Who can endure the heat of his anger?
His wrath is poured out like fire,
and the rocks are broken asunder by him.
The LORD is good,
a stronghold in the day of trouble;
he knows those who take refuge in him.

NAHUM 1:6–7

Opening Prayer

Heavenly Father,
source of all justice,
destroyer of all wickedness,
we turn to you with confidence.
We confess and repent of our sins.
We seek your mercy.
Save us from distress.
Deliver us from evil.
Strengthen our hearts to love you.
Through Christ our Lord.
Amen.

Basic Message

God will allow violent and evil people to suffer the consequences
of their sins.

Introductory Overview

The Book of Nahum is a collection of the prophet's preaching and warnings. In particular, Nahum teaches that the fall of Nineveh, the capital of the Assyrian Empire, is an image of the consequences of sin.

Basic Outline

The Book of Nahum consists of three chapters:

- Chapter 1: God's judgment on Assyria and on his own people.
- Chapters 2–3: The fall of Nineveh.

Application to Our Lives

In Nahum 1, the prophet describes a dreadful scene in which God's wrath — his justice — is brought upon the violent and the wicked. Nahum uses the image of the Assyrian Empire to show the full effects of God's justice, as the empire crumbles, and its capital city is destroyed. In the midst of this description, however, Nahum reminds us that God is good — a stronghold and a refuge for those who turn to him. In summary, God's justice is given only to those who reject his mercy.

The arrogant and the proud think that they do not need God. They reject his moral law, his commands to care for the poor, and his summons to be gracious and kind. The proud use manipulation, fear, and violence to impose control over others; such arrogance calls for God's justice.

In our lives, we are reminded that God loves us and desires to be our Savior rather than our judge. He is an ocean of mercy and desires to show us his compassion and kindness. In our sinfulness and fallenness, we can turn to him as a stronghold and refuge in our guilt and distress. If we harden our hearts, however, and allow pride to consume us, God will show his love for us as our Judge. Whether God shows us his love as Savior or as Judge, the choice is ours.

Basic Points

Author: The Jewish and Christian traditions attribute the Book of Nahum to the prophet Nahum, although other writers and editors worked on the book.

Placement: Nahum is the forty-first book of the Old Testament. It is part of what are called the prophetic books of the Bible. Nahum is a supplemental book of the principal narrative books of the Bible.

Keywords:

- The ruins of Nineveh: Like Sodom and Gomorrah, the term is used to describe the justice of God and the consequences of sin.

Getting Started

The Book of Nahum is an account of the prophet's preaching and warnings. In particular, it recounts Nahum's use of the fall of the Assyrian Empire to teach the consequences of sin. It consists of three chapters and so can be easily read in its entirety in one sitting, but here are some passages to help us: good news for Judah (1:12–15) and the rejoicing of the righteous as wickedness is defeated (3:19).

Concluding Prayer

Eternal God,
ever-living and all-powerful,
we are nothing without you.
Show us your mercy and kindness.

We repent of our sins.
We ask your pardon.
Accept us. Protect us.
Be our stronghold and refuge,
for we need you.
Heal our brokenness. Restore us.
Show us your glory.
Through Christ our Lord.
Amen.

Habakkuk

Woe to him who heaps up what is not his own —
for how long? —
and loads himself with pledges!

HABAKKUK 2:6B

Opening Prayer
Eternal God,
Lord of all,
hear our prayer.
Listen to our supplications.
Bring peace to our land.
Allow justice to flourish.
Protect the vulnerable and the weak.
Deliver us from evil.
Show us your glory.
Through Christ our Lord.
Amen.

Basic Message
God does not create or desire evil, but he allows it so that a greater good can come to us.

Introductory Overview
The Book of Habakkuk is unique among the prophetic books. Rather than a collection of preaching and warnings, it is a record of the prayer of the prophet before God. It shows us the sorrow

and supplication of a righteous person over the evils of his day.

Basic Outline
The Book of Habakkuk consists of three parts:

- Chapters 1–2:4: The dialogue between Habakkuk and God over evil.
- Chapter 2:5–20: The five woes of God against those who do evil.
- Chapter 3: The prophet's prayer of confidence and trust in God.

Application to Our Lives
In Habakkuk 2, God pronounces five woes for the evil in Habakkuk's day. The woes included unjust business practices, taking advantage of the poor, slave labor, the abuse of alcohol, and idolatry. While each of these is a good reminder for our own day, we need to focus on unjust business practices, especially taking outrageous interest on loans to the poor. God severely denounces this practice because it further enslaves the poor and does not allow them to be freed from their debt. It makes the rich richer and greatly burdens the poor.

In our lives as God's children, the Lord's wisdom reminds us through Habakkuk that our task is to help and console those in need. We must not take advantage of someone in dire straits. We should not add more weight to those struggling to provide for themselves and their families. Our task is to lighten their loads, doing our best to help and encourage those in need. Whether this means lending money or privately owned property or supporting public programs, we are called to offer reasonable help. We are never to take advantage of those in need.

Basic Points

Author: The Jewish and Christian traditions attribute the Book of Habakkuk to the prophet Habakkuk, although other writers and editors worked on the book.

Placement: Habakkuk is the forty-second book of the Old Testament. It is part of what are called the prophetic books of the Bible. Habakkuk is a supplemental book of the principal narrative books of the Bible.

Keywords:

- Watchman: The prophet Habakkuk identifies himself as a watchman. He stands waiting for God to answer his prayer. The image is symbolic of heartfelt and persistent prayer.

Getting Started

The Book of Habakkuk provides the prayerful supplication of a prophet to God over the evils in his day. It consists of three chapters. While the eventual goal is to read the book in its entirety, here are some passages to help us: the prophet's prayer in his distress (1:2); Habakkuk's request that God repeat some of his powerful signs that were done earlier in salvation history (3:2); and the prophet's declaration of trust in God, no matter what happens (3:17–19).

Concluding Prayer

Good and gracious God,
you hear our prayers;
you bless us with wisdom.
Give us your strength.
Scatter the darkness.

Vanquish evil.
Help us to follow you.
Keep us faithful.
We trust in you.
Through Christ our Lord.
Amen.

Zephaniah

Neither their silver nor their gold
shall be able to deliver them
on the day of the wrath of the LORD.
In the fire of his jealous wrath,
all the earth shall be consumed;
for a full, yes, sudden end
he will make of all the inhabitants of the earth.

ZEPHANIAH 1:18

Opening Prayer

Eternal Father,
you hear the cry of the poor.
Listen to our appeal,
for you are our only hope.
Have mercy on our sins.
Restore us to your grace.
Grant us your salvation.
Show us your glory.
Through Christ our Lord.
Amen.

Basic Message

God judges evil but brings salvation to the righteous.

Introductory Overview

The Book of Zephaniah is a collection of the preaching, prophecies, and visions of the prophet Zephaniah. In particular, Zephaniah warns of judgment upon Jerusalem and all the nations because of their rebellion and wickedness. He is preaching at the end of the southern kingdom (Judah) but before the invasion by Babylon. Zephaniah prophesizes the coming of the Babylonians and promises a new beginning to the remnant — those who are faithful to God.

Basic Outline
The Book of Zephaniah consists of three parts:

- Chapters 1–2:3: God's judgment upon Jerusalem.
- Chapters 2:4—3:8: God's judgment upon all the nations.
- Chapters 3:9–20: The future hope of Jerusalem and the nations.

Application to Our Lives
In Zephaniah 1, God denounces the sins and wickedness of his people. He tells them of his impending day of judgment. In the many punishments that will befall them, their gold and silver will provide no help for they will be destroyed with them.

The denunciations of gold and silver are important because these were often used in pagan worship, and their collection often meant that the poor were neglected. In effect, the justice of God — which calls for true worship and care for the poor — was ignored.

In our lives, we have to be careful about the accumulation of wealth. Wealth lies to us and promises us a false security. Many unbelievers put their confidence and their future in the hands of their money. As the children of God, we have to put God first and give generously in worship. We also must have a heart for the poor and others in need. If we have an abundance of wealth, we must ask hard questions about how we can use it to serve those in need.

Basic Points
Author: The Jewish and Christian traditions attribute the Book of Zephaniah to the prophet Zephaniah, although other writers and editors worked on the book.

Placement: Zephaniah is the forty-third book of the Old Testament. It is part of what are called the prophetic books of the Bible. Zephaniah is a supplemental book of the principal narrative books of the Bible.

Keywords:

- Baal: A pagan deity that was popularly worshiped by many people throughout salvation history. God's people periodically fell into idolatry through the worship of this false god.

Getting Started
The Book of Zephaniah is a collection of the preaching, prophecies, and visions of the prophet. It consists of three chapters. While the eventual goal is to read the book in its entirety, here are some passages to help us: the salvation of the humble (2:1–3); the unity of all nations in the worship of the true God (3:9–10); and God as a warrior for his people (3:16–19).

Concluding Prayer
O mighty warrior,
Prince of Peace, Wonderful Counselor,
hear our petitions.
We denounce our idols.

We abandon the false gods.
We turn to you.
Purify our hearts.
Cleanse us of our sins.
Keep us faithful to you.
Through Christ our Lord.
Amen.

Haggai

You have looked for much, and behold, it came to little; and when you brought it home, I blew it away. Why? says the LORD of hosts. Because of my house that lies in ruins, while you busy yourselves each with his own house.

HAGGAI 1:9

Opening Prayer
Everlasting Father,
we praise you. We bless you.
You are above all things.
You alone are holy.
You alone are worthy of our devotion.
We turn to you. We adore you alone.
Help us to build the temples of our hearts.
Strengthen us with your grace.
Raise up our worship. Make it worthy.
Help us to serve you.
Show us your glory.
Through Christ our Lord.
Amen.

Basic Message
God desires us to praise him, so that he can purify us and give us his blessings.

Introductory Overview
The Book of Haggai is a collection of the preaching, prophecies, and visions of the prophet Haggai. He is preaching to God's
people as they return to Jerusalem after the Babylonian Exile.
Haggai is exhorting the people to abandon their self-interests
and rebuild the Temple.

Basic Outline
The Book of Haggai consists of four parts:

- Chapter 1: Accusations against the infidelities and
  selfishness of God's people and the command to
  build the Second Temple.
- Chapter 2:1–9: The disappointment over the Second Temple and the promises for a future Temple.
- Chapter 2:10–19: The call to fidelity to God's covenant.
- Chapter 2:20–23: The future hope of God's kingdom.

Application to Our Lives
In Haggai 1, God admonishes his people. They are living in
splendid homes while the Temple remains unbuilt. God tells his
people that he has not blessed them because of their obstinacy in
refusing to rebuild the Temple and failing to worship him rightly.
The people have been distracted. Their own material wealth has
taken over their hearts. God calls them out of their selfishness
and redirects their focus to the Temple and true worship.

In our lives, it's easy to focus on our own houses. Whether it's
our actual physical homes with things to fix, repair, and decorate,
or the various duties and responsibilities of our lives, we want
our "houses" to be well ordered and beautiful. While this focus
can be a good thing, it becomes a spiritual distraction when the

"house" of the Lord — namely, our soul — has not been fixed, repaired, or decorated with God's grace. We have to make sure that our souls are worthy to host the presence of God. The other things of life — however important they are — should always flow from these most important things: the right worship of God and the care of our souls. If we bypass right worship and the beauty of our souls, and instead worry about everything else in our lives, then we miss the most preeminent tasks of our lives. And the passing things of this world also lose their meaning and value. The people of Haggai's day lost this focus. We have to be attentive so that we won't lose it.

Basic Points

Author: The Jewish and Christian traditions attribute the Book of Haggai to the prophet Haggai, although other writers and editors worked on the book.

Placement: Haggai is the forty-fourth book of the Old Testament. It is part of what are called the prophetic books of the Bible. Haggai is a supplemental book of the principal narrative books of the Bible.

Keywords:

- Zerubbabel: One of the leaders of God's people after the Babylonian Exile. He led the effort to build and consecrate the Second Temple. As a descendant of King David, he is presented as an image of the future Anointed Savior. He is highly praised in the Book of Haggai.

Getting Started

The Book of Haggai is a collection of the preaching, prophecies, and visions of the prophet. It consists of two chapters and deals exclusively with the building of the Second Temple and a future Temple of glory. While the eventual goal is to read the book in its entirety, here are some passages to help us: Haggai's call as a prophet (1:1); the promise of a future glorious Temple (2:9); and the continuation of King David's line (2:23).

Concluding Prayer

O mighty warrior,
Prince of Peace, Wonderful Counselor,
hear our petitions.
We denounce our idols.
We abandon the false gods.
We turn to you.
Purify our hearts.
Cleanse us of our sins.
Keep us faithful to you.
Through Christ our Lord.
Amen.

Zechariah

Rejoice greatly, O daughter of Zion!
  Shout aloud, O daughter of Jerusalem!
Behold, your king comes to you;
  triumphant and victorious is he,
humble and riding on a donkey,
  on a colt the foal of a donkey.

ZECHARIAH 9:9

Opening Prayer

Eternal Father,
Maker of promises,
Source of all fulfillment,
you are glorious and without deception.
You guide us and lead us in unexpected ways.
You call us to trust you.
We surrender to you.
We rely on you alone.
Strengthen us with your grace.
Show us your glory.
Through Christ our Lord.
Amen.

Basic Message

God fulfills his promises on his time. He uses creative and unexpected ways to bring about such fulfillment.

Introductory Overview

The Book of Zechariah is a collection of the preaching, prophecies, and dream-visions of the prophet Zechariah. He is preaching to God's people as they return to Jerusalem after the Babylonian Exile. He is answering the inquiry: Where is the fulfillment of the glorious promises God made to our ancestors? Why do we not have the Anointed Savior and the New Jerusalem? The prophet responds that the fulfillment of God's promises will come at a future time. The splendor of such fulfillment cannot be imagined.

Basic Outline

The Book of Zechariah consists of three main parts:

- Chapters 1–8: The prophet's call to repentance and his multiple dream-visions.
- Chapters 9–11: Images of the future Anointed Savior.
- Chapters 12–14: Images of the future kingdom of God's people.

Application to Our Lives

In Zechariah 9, God describes the future Anointed King, one who will be everything anyone could hope for. He will be a mighty Savior and the Giver of every good blessing. And yet, though powerful, he will also be profoundly humble. He will not be proud or arrogant.

As an expression of his humility, the Anointed Savior will come to us riding on a donkey. He will not enter Jerusalem on a strong stallion or military chariot. He will come humbly as both servant of God and king. This prophecy is later fulfilled in salvation history when Jesus Christ enters Jerusalem on a donkey.

In our lives, we have to pay attention to how we exercise the authority and power we've received. Whether it's as parents to our children, employers to our workers, civil leaders to citizens, or in any other context, the power we've received is a gift from God. We must use it lightly and with great humility. Zechariah reminds us that God rejects the proud. Our Anointed Savior, who is Lord of all, demonstrates this humility for us. As God's people, we are called to imitate his example and be people of humility and meekness.

Basic Points

Author: The Jewish and Christian traditions attribute the Book of Zechariah to the prophet Zechariah, although other writers and editors worked on the book.

Placement: Zechariah is the forty-fifth book of the Old Testament. It is part of what are called the prophetic books of the Bible. Zechariah is a supplemental book of the principal narrative books of the Bible.

Keywords:

- Joseph: The high priest in Jerusalem after the Babylonian Exile. He leads the consecration of the Second Temple and works closely with Zerubbabel in reestablishing Jerusalem. He is depicted in the Book of Zechariah as symbolic of the future Anointed Savior.
- Dream interpretation: In various parts of the Bible, dreams are interpreted for wisdom. Such a practice is very different from sorcery. Sorcery sees a dream as its own source of meaning. In biblical dream interpretation, God speaks through a dream, and so the focus is to discern his divine wisdom. Such in-

terpretation relies on God's covenant and his public revelation and teachings.

Getting Started

The Book of Zechariah is a collection of the preaching, prophecies, and dream-visions of the prophet. It consists of fourteen chapters and, following the Babylonian Exile, stresses the importance of rebuilding the Second Temple in Jerusalem. While the eventual goal is to read the book in its entirety, here are some passages to help us: the call of God to return to him (1:1–5); the crowning of the mysterious "Branch" figure (6:9–15); and the mourning for the Pierced One (12:10–14).

Concluding Prayer

O God,
you are a mighty Savior
who always seeks to bless us.
Come to our assistance.
Guide us along your path for us.
Give us a greater hope in you.
Help us to place our trust in you alone.
We turn to you.
Show us your glory.
Through Christ our Lord.
Amen.

Malachi

For I hate divorce, says the LORD the God of Israel, and covering one's garment with violence, says the LORD of hosts. So take heed to yourselves and do not be faithless.

MALACHI 2:16

Opening Prayer
Father of lights,
you point us to your glory.
You call us to be prepared.
Mold and shape us by your grace.
Help us to wait for you.
We look for your day above all others.
Keep us faithful to you.
Show us your glory.
Through Christ our Lord.
Amen.

Basic Message
God calls us to worship. If we worship him with a pure heart, he will bless us and let us share in his glory.

Introductory Overview
The Book of Malachi is a collection of the preaching and arguments of the prophet Malachi. The format of the book follows a "claim-disagreement" exchange between God and his people. The prophet receives both claims and disagreements, and he

seeks to explain the wisdom of God and his expectations for his people. Malachi is preaching after the Babylonian Exile. He is addressing the sorrows and disappointments of God's people, while also revealing God's answers to their concerns.

Basic Outline
The Book of Malachi consists of two parts:

- Chapters 1–4:3: Six "claim-disagreement" exchanges between God and his people.
- Chapter 4:4–5: The future glory of God's people.

Application to Our Lives
In Malachi 2, God denounces divorce. He uses the strong language of "hate" when it comes to the practice. The context of the passage is helpful. At the time of Malachi, many of the men among God's people had married pagan women and had divorced their legitimate Jewish wives to do so. Consequently, these men did not worship the true God and were outside of the blessings of his covenant. Malachi exhorts them to repent and return to their true wives — the wives of their youth. Marriage must be honored. Spouses need to work things out and persevere in their love for each other.

While the context is helpful, the teaching goes beyond the historical setting. God does not want his people to suffer. Divorce causes immense suffering in the hearts of people, particularly children. God does not want his people to undergo this heartache. He hates sin and the suffering that comes from it. Oftentimes the people who most agree with this teaching are those who have gone through a divorce. They know the agony and hurt that comes with it. It's something they never imagined or anticipated in their lives. Sometimes a civil divorce has merit, but it's never preferred and never something that people plan for or want in their lives.

Those who are discerning marriage and those who are called to the sacred marital covenant should remind themselves of how seriously God takes marriage. Although our culture can treat marriage like a commodity, God does not. He calls one man and one woman to be together for life. Spouses are called to do everything possible to love and honor each other for as long as they both shall live. This is not an easy way of life. But to those who are called to married life — and those who are open to living it faithfully and generously — God provides his strength. He gives his grace.

Basic Points

Author: The Jewish and Christian traditions attribute the Book of Malachi to the prophet Malachi, although other writers and editors worked on the book.

Placement: Malachi is the forty-sixth book of the Old Testament. It is part of what are called the prophetic books of the Bible. Malachi is a supplemental book of the principal narrative books of the Bible.

Keywords:

- Elijah: Malachi tells us that Elijah will return before the Anointed Savior comes. This is not a promise of reincarnation but a spiritual reference. The spirit of Elijah will come before the Anointed Savior. This is fulfilled later in salvation history by St. John the Baptist, who had Elijah's spirit and zeal.
- Lord of Hosts: The military title for God throughout salvation history, since "hosts" is a reference to military units. The title points to God's power and

strength. Whenever the title is used, some type of warfare — physical or spiritual — is indicated. The title is used throughout the Book of Malachi.

Getting Started

The Book of Malachi is a collection of the preaching and warnings of the prophet. It consists of four chapters and addresses the disappointment of God's people after their return to Jerusalem following the Babylonian Exile. While the eventual goal is to read the book in its entirety, here are some passages to help us: the confusion of God's people (2:17); the coming messenger (3:1); and the reward of those who are faithful to God (4:1–3).

Concluding Prayer

Sun of righteousness,
come and rise in our hearts.
Enlighten our paths.
Show us your way.
Keep us faithful to you.
Spare us from your judgment.
Help us to love you.
Teach us to worship you.
Show us your glory.
Through Christ our Lord.
Amen.

NEW TESTAMENT

The Life and Teachings
of the Anointed Savior
and the Witness of
the Early Church

The Gospels

Matthew
Mark
Luke
John

Gospel of Matthew

As Jesus passed on from there, he saw a man called Matthew sitting at the tax office; and he said to him, "Follow me." And he rose and followed him.

Matthew 9:9

Opening Prayer

Heavenly Father,
you sent us your Son as the Anointed Savior.
We praise you. We love you.
Grant us your salvation.
Help us to follow your way.
Keep us faithful.
Show us your glory.
Through Christ our Lord.
Amen.

Basic Message

Jesus of Nazareth is the eternal Son of God and the long-awaited Anointed Savior. He fulfills all the prophecies and promises of God and is the new Moses and the new David.

Introductory Overview

Matthew's Gospel shows us that Jesus of Nazareth is God-made-man and the Anointed Savior of salvation history. Matthew also shows the Lord Jesus as the new Moses, initiating a New Covenant with the Father, as well as the son of David, foretold in the

Old Testament, who will establish God's kingdom forever. Matthew is aimed at a Jewish Christian audience. It provides biblical evidence that Jesus is the fulfillment of the entire Old Testament and thus truly the anticipated Anointed Savior.

Basic Outline
The Gospel of Matthew has seven main parts:

- Chapters 1–2: Jesus' birth and early life.
- Chapters 3–7: The foundation of God's kingdom.
- Chapters 8–10: The proclamation of God's kingdom.
- Chapters 11–13:53: The mystery of God's kingdom.
- Chapters 13:54—18: The kingdom on earth — the Church.
- Chapters 19–25: The coming of the eternal kingdom.
- Chapters 26–28: The passion, death, and resurrection of Jesus Christ.

Application to Our Lives
In Matthew 9:9–13, we are given a brief autobiography of the author. Matthew, who was also called Levi, was a tax collector. Tax collectors were members of God's people who sold out their own by collecting taxes for Rome, an unbelieving and brutal occupying force. Tax collectors were known to be corrupt, routinely overcharging on taxes. As such, tax collectors were generally looked upon as sinners and traitors to their people. Matthew was a despised and ostracized member of society.

The Lord Jesus comes to Matthew while he is sitting at his tax booth, and he calls him to himself. Matthew hears the call and immediately follows Jesus.

In our lives, we can allow sin to define us and the consequences of sin to overwhelm us. We can find ourselves on the peripheries of life and think there's no hope. The Lord Jesus, however, accepts no restrictions and refuses any barrier in seeking us out. As he went to Matthew's tax booth, the very source of his corruption and sin, so he comes to us. He calls to us, "Follow me!" He summons us out of darkness and into his own wonderful light. We must hear his call, trust him, and immediately abandon our sin and follow him.

Basic Points

Author: The Christian tradition attributes the Gospel of Matthew to the apostle Matthew (also called Levi).

Placement: The Gospel of Matthew is the first book of the New Testament and the forty-seventh of the Bible. It is the first of four Gospel Books.

Keywords:

- Jewish Christian: A believer in Jesus Christ who came from the tradition of the Old Testament. Along with the Gentile Christians, they were one of two major groups in the early Church.
- Messiah: A Hebrew word meaning "Anointed Savior." The Greek word for "messiah" is *christ*. The entire Old Testament was a preparation for the coming of the Anointed Savior.
- Gospel: The life and teachings of Jesus Christ. The Gospel is contained in four Gospel Books within the Christian tradition. The word literally means "good news."

Getting Started

While the eventual goal is to read all twenty-eight chapters of the Gospel of Matthew, here are three selections that can get us started. Each selection shows us the depth and wisdom of Matthew: the Beatitudes as a path to happiness and holiness (5:1–12); the healing of the servant of the centurion, whose humble words of supplication have been adapted for use at Mass (8:5–13); and the Great Commission, which calls us to share the Good News with all people (28:16–20).

Concluding Prayer
Lord Jesus,
you are the Son of the living God;
you are the Son of David;
you are the Anointed Savior.
We have waited for you.
We run to you. We need you.
You are our only hope.
Cast out our fear.
Show us your strength and mercy.
Grant us your salvation.
For you are Lord forever and ever.
Amen.

Gospel of Mark

And immediately he left the synagogue, and entered the house of Simon and Andrew, with James and John. Now Simon's mother-in-law lay sick with a fever, and immediately they told him of her. And he came and took her by the hand and lifted her up, and the fever left her; and she served them.

MARK 1:29–31

Opening Prayer

Lord Jesus,
your love and mercy are beyond our understanding.
You have sought us out.
You come to ransom us from sin.
You desire to share your life with us.
We thank you for your loving kindness.
We praise you.
We rejoice in your grace.
Show us your glory.
For you are Lord forever and ever.
Amen.

Basic Message

Jesus of Nazareth is the Son of God, the anticipated Anointed Savior of salvation history. He does not come in worldly power or with stately influence. He comes to us as a suffering servant.

Introductory Overview

Mark's Gospel shows us that Jesus of Nazareth is the eternal Son of God and the long-awaited Anointed Savior of salvation history. Mark emphasizes the Lord Jesus as God's suffering servant. As the shortest of the Gospel Books, Mark is not as developed as the others. It's brief and to the point. Mark was written in Rome and is aimed at a Gentile Christian audience who were in the midst of a severe persecution as Christian believers. Mark's emphasis on the sufferings of the Lord Jesus were meant to console and inspire the early Christians in their own sufferings and torment for their faith in Jesus Christ.

Basic Outline

The Gospel of Mark has three main parts:

- Chapters 1–6:29: The Lord's ministry and teachings in Galilee.
- Chapters 6:30—10: The journeys and teachings of the Lord Jesus.
- Chapters 11–16: The Passion, death, and resurrection of Jesus Christ.

Application to Our Lives

As we see in Mark's Gospel, the Lord Jesus knows the fallenness of the world and the suffering that comes with it. He knows the vulnerability, distress, and anxiety that we feel when we're sick or injured. In Mark 1:29–31, we read the endearing story of Saint Peter's mother-in-law. Upon entering the house of his apostles and friends, the Lord Jesus was told of her illness. Immediately he went to her. He did not leave when he heard that a sick person was in the house. He did not avoid her, nor was he unconcerned or unsettled. Instead, the Lord directly went to serve her. He took her by the hand, lifted her up, and healed her. His first response was one of presence, compassion, and accompaniment.

In our lives, we will suffer illnesses, as will those around us. While we may never work a miraculous healing, we can go to the sick, spend time with them, hold their hand, pray with them, and give them the warmth of our love and accompaniment. Often-times, the sick are treated with disdain and neglected. People are either afraid or too busy to give them any attention. As followers of the Lord Jesus, we are called to slow down, get over any fear we might have, and selflessly serve and spend time with the sick and the suffering.

Basic Points

Author: The Christian tradition attributes the Gospel of Mark to the disciple John Mark, who was a cousin of Barnabas and companion of Saint Paul. Mark was also an interpreter for Saint Peter.

Placement: The Gospel of Mark is the second book of the New Testament and the forty-eighth book of the Bible. It is the second of four Gospel Books.

Keywords:

- Gentile Christian: A believer in Jesus Christ who was not from the Old Testament tradition and who often left a background of idolatry and unbelief to follow the living God. Along with the Jewish Chris-tians, they were one of two major groups in the early Church.
- Suffering: The means by which the Anointed Sav-ior brought about the redemption of humanity. The Lord Jesus invites his disciples to share in his suffer-ings and unite their own sufferings with his, as he

seeks to save all people.

- Galilee: The northern region of the Promised Land during the time of the Lord Jesus. It was his home region and was the place where most of his public ministry took place.

Getting Started

The Gospel of Mark is the shortest of the four Gospel Books. While the eventual goal is to read all sixteen chapters of the Gospel Book, here are three selections that can get us started. Each selection shows us the depth and wisdom of Mark: the Lord Jesus' healing of the paralytic who is loved and served by faithful friends (2:1–12); the Lord Jesus' sleeping during a great storm (4:35–41); and the Transfiguration of the Lord Jesus, which gives us a glimpse of the glory of his divinity (9:1–8).

Concluding Prayer

Lord Jesus,
Anointed Savior and Suffering Servant,
you come to us in our infirmities.
Heal us. Save us.
Make us instruments of your grace.
Bless us with your love and courage.
Help us to go to the sick and those in need.
Show us your glory.
For you are Lord forever and ever.
Amen.

Gospel of Luke

But God said to him, "Fool! This night your soul is required of you; and the things you have prepared, whose will they be?" So is he who lays up treasure for himself, and is not rich toward God.

LUKE 12:20–21

Opening Prayer

Lord Jesus,
God of mercy,
you turn to us in our need.
You are the Anointed Savior of all.
Come to us. We trust in you.
We repent.
Show us the face of the Father.
Grant us your salvation.
For you are Lord forever and ever.
Amen.

Basic Message

Jesus of Nazareth is the God-Man and the promised Anointed Savior for all humanity. The Lord's gift of salvation is offered to all people.

Introductory Overview

Luke's Gospel shows us that Jesus of Nazareth is the Son of God and the Savior of humanity. Luke was a Gentile, not from the Old

Testament tradition of God's people, so his perspective is unique among the Gospel writers. He emphasizes the love and mercy of the Lord Jesus for all human beings and so stresses that the gift of salvation is offered to everyone. As a medical doctor accustomed to caring for the sick, Luke was sensitive to the Lord's tenderness toward those who suffer and his kindness to the vulnerable, and he highlighted these in his Gospel.

Basic Outline
The Gospel of Luke has four main parts:

- Chapters 1–2: The early life of the Lord Jesus.
- Chapters 3–9:50: The Lord's ministry in Galilee.
- Chapters 9:51—21: The Lord's journey and ministry in Jerusalem.
- Chapters 22–24: The passion, death, and resurrection of Jesus Christ.

Application to Our Lives
In Luke 12:13–21, the Lord Jesus gives us the parable of the rich fool. This parable shows us the consequences of selfishness and calls us to generosity. In the parable, the rich fool is blessed with abundance. In his surplus, however, he thinks only of himself. With no intention of sharing, he hoards his goods and builds bigger barns to store them in. But then his life is taken from him, and his goods can no longer provide him any benefit.

In our lives, we can hoard the good things of this earth and use God's blessings only to give ourselves more comfort and ease. We live in a material world, and it's easy to let its spirit take over our hearts. The Gospel reminds us, however, that divine blessings are given to us so that we can be blessings to others. Because we are disciples, our hearts belong to the Lord Jesus and to our neighbors, especially to those in need. Rather than store up treasures for ourselves on earth, we are to imitate the Lord Jesus by generously giving our lives and resources in selfless service to others.

Basic Points

Author: The Christian tradition attributes the Gospel of Luke to Luke, the disciple of Saint Paul, who is also referred to as "the beloved physician" (Col 4:14).

Placement: The Gospel of Luke is the third book of the New Testament and the forty-ninth book of the Bible. It is the third of four Gospel Books. Luke is the thirteenth of the principal narrative books of the Bible. (See Appendix A.)

Keywords:

- Greco-Roman culture: The predominant culture at the time of the Lord Jesus. It was overwhelmingly at odds with the worship, message, and way of life of God's people. Saint Luke presents the Gospel in a way that would appeal to the people of this culture.
- Parable: A simple or creative story that is used to teach a moral or spiritual lesson. Parables were regularly used by the Lord Jesus in his public teachings.

Getting Started

While the eventual goal is to read all twenty-four chapters of the Gospel of Luke, here are three selections that can get us started. Each selection shows us the depth and wisdom of Luke: the parable of the Good Samaritan and our call to care for one another (10:25–37); the famous parable of the prodigal son and our summons to show mercy to one another (15:11–32); and the story of the rich man and Lazarus and the command to care for the poor and the suffering (16:19–31). Of the four Gospel Books, only Luke gives us these three stories of the Lord Jesus. They illustrate Luke's unique emphasis on mercy and kindness as he shares the Gospel in a culture outside the Old Testament tradition.

Concluding Prayer

Lord Jesus,
you are the eternal God.
You are the author of our salvation.
You are the Lord and Savior of all.
Come to us.
Grant us your salvation.
Help us to give your mercy to others.
Show us your glory.
For you are Lord forever and ever.
Amen.

Gospel of John

If I then, your Lord and Teacher, have washed your feet, you also ought to wash one another's feet. For I have given you an example, that you also should do as I have done to you.

John 13:14–15

Opening Prayer

Lord Jesus,
you are the everlasting Temple,
the presence of God among us.
We turn to you with confidence.
Show us your love.
Give us your grace.
Grant us your salvation.
Open our minds and hearts to you.
Reveal your glory.
For you are Lord forever and ever.
Amen.

Basic Message

Jesus of Nazareth is the word of God made flesh. He is the promised Anointed Savior, the only Son of God, who reveals the Father to us. He is the everlasting Temple.

Introductory Overview

John's Gospel strongly emphasizes Jesus of Nazareth as the eternal Son of God, the living Temple, and the only way for humanity to know God the Father. This Gospel is different from the others — Matthew, Mark, and Luke — since it follows a different pattern. The other Gospel Books are structured in a relatively similar way, stressing the journeys of the Lord Jesus in his public ministry and his teachings on the way of life to his disciples. John, however, is of the priestly class of God's people. As such, he follows the liturgical year of the Temple and shows the Lord Jesus as the fulfillment of the words and deeds of God as displayed in the feast days of God's people. John ultimately presents the Lord as the living Temple, the presence of God on earth. As such, he reveals Jesus of Nazareth as the only Son of God and the long-awaited Anointed Savior.

Basic Outline
The Gospel of John has four main parts:

- Chapter 1:1–18: Prologue.
- Chapters 1:19—12: The Book of Signs, containing seven miracles, or "signs," that show the Lord Jesus as God-made-man and the fulfillment of the Old Testament.
- Chapters 13–20: The Book of Glory, which contains Christ's teaching and actions at the Last Supper and an extensive account of his passion, death, and resurrection.
- Chapter 21: Post-Resurrection appearances and commission.

Application to Our Lives
In John 13:1–20, we have the narrative of the Lord Jesus washing the feet of his apostles. Jesus thereby gives us the perfect example of selfless service, as well as the new commandment to love one another as he has loved us. The heart of discipleship is serving

in ways that demand sacrifice and a true spiritual death to ourselves. The Lord Jesus washed the feet of all his apostles, even Judas, who he knew would betray him that very night.

In our lives, we can ignore others or condition our service and refuse to truly serve. It's easy to focus on ourselves and make sure we have whatever we want (or think we need). We can also be deceived and appease our guilt by giving just a little or by serving only within our comfort zone. Our call, however, is to imitate the Lord Jesus and to serve by rolling up our sleeves, washing some dirty feet, and humbling ourselves by caring for others with a selfless and sacrificial heart.

Basic Points

Author: The Christian tradition attributes the Gospel of John to the apostle John, brother of James and son of Zebedee; John is also called "the Beloved" (see 13:23).

Placement: The Gospel of John is the fourth book of the New Testament and the fiftieth book of the Bible. It is the fourth of four Gospel Books.

Keywords:

- Synoptic Gospels: The Gospel Books of Matthew, Mark, and Luke. The word "synoptic" means "one vision" and refers here to the first three Gospel Books, because they follow a similar pattern in presenting the Gospel.
- Liturgical year: The annual calendar of major feast days that celebrate the words and deeds of God throughout salvation history.

Getting Started

While the eventual goal is to read all twenty-one chapters of the Gospel of John, here are three selections that can get us started. Each selection shows us the depth and wisdom of John: the Wedding at Cana and the Lord Jesus' love for and obedience to his mother (2:1–12); the Lord Jesus' conversation with the Samaritan woman at Jacob's well, the longest recorded exchange between Jesus and another person in Scripture (4:1–42); and the Lord Jesus' declaring himself the Good Shepherd (10:1–18).

Concluding Prayer

Lord Jesus,
you are the presence of God, the eternal Temple.
You are the only Son of God and our loving Savior.
You gave us your sacred Body and Blood as our food and drink.
You set before us the perfect example of selfless love.
You call us to follow you.
Grant us your grace.
Give us your strength.
We love you. We adore you.
For you are Lord forever and ever.
Amen.

Historical Book

Acts of the Apostles

Acts of the Apostles

And they held steadfastly to the apostles' teaching and fellowship, to the breaking of the bread and to the prayers.

ACTS 2:42

Opening Prayer

Lord Jesus,
God of love and mercy,
we thank you for the gift of the Church.
You have united what was scattered.
You have healed what was broken.
May we always be faithful to you.
Send us your Holy Spirit.
May we seek your kingdom above all things.
Help us to share your Good News.
Grant us your salvation.
For you are Lord forever and ever.
Amen.

Basic Message

The Holy Spirit empowers the Church of Jesus Christ to build the kingdom of God through the ministry of the apostles.

Introductory Overview

The Acts of the Apostles gives us a broad summary of the growth of the Church, from the Lord Jesus' resurrection and ascension to the first Roman imprisonment of Saint Paul. The Book of Acts shows us the Church of Christ as the new assembly of God's people and narrates the expansion of the Church by the power of the Holy Spirit.

Basic Outline

The Acts of the Apostles has five main parts:

- Chapter 1: The Ascension of the Lord Jesus and apostolic succession.
- Chapters 2—8:3: The Church in Jerusalem.
- Chapters 8:4—9: The apostles in Judea and Samaria.
- Chapters 10—15:35: The mission to the Gentiles.
- Chapters 15:36—28: Saint Paul's mission to the world.

Application to Our Lives

Throughout chapter 2 of the Acts of the Apostles, we are given a wonderful description of the closeness of the early Church. In every way, the members sought to continue "the Way" of the Lord Jesus and were devoted to it. The early disciples were attentive and faithful to apostolic teaching; they received the sacraments, prayed, shared holy fellowship, and worked together to serve the poor. In all these ways, they wanted to live as the Lord Jesus lived and to love as he loved.

In our lives, the Way of the Lord Jesus remains the same. Our lives, homes, and parishes should resemble this way of life. It's difficult to retain this way of life in our world today. We are all very mobile, transient, filled with commitments, stretched in our schedules, and entrenched in our sense of independence. And yet our discipleship calls us to a particular way of life. As the early Church made the Way of the Lord a priority, so should we. Each of us needs to slow things down, refocus our hearts, review again the Way of the Lord Jesus, and zealously recommit ourselves to it.

Basic Points

Author: The Christian tradition attributes the Acts of the Apostles to Luke, disciple of Saint Paul.

Placement: The Acts of the Apostles is the fifth book of the New Testament and the fifty-first book of the Bible. The Acts of the Apostles is the fourteenth of the principal narrative books of the Bible. (See Appendix A.)

Keywords:

- Ascension: The event in which the Lord Jesus — with his human and Divine Nature — returned to the right hand of the Father. In his Ascension, the Lord Jesus entrusted his saving mission to his Church, under the leadership of the apostles and their successors.
- Apostolic succession: The continuity of selected men holding the established office of the apostles. It shows that the work of the apostles did not end with their deaths. When one apostle died, a successor was chosen to continue the work of the Gospel. Such a succession is seen when Matthias is selected to take Judas's place among the apostles (see 1:12–26).
- Pentecost: The coming of the Holy Spirit upon Mary and the apostles. Devotionally, it's called the birthday of the Church, since the Holy Spirit invigorated the apostles to fulfill the commission of the Lord Jesus to preach and continue his saving work throughout the world.

Getting Started

While the eventual goal is to read all twenty-eight chapters of the Acts of the Apostles, here are three selections that can get us started. Each selection shows us the depth and wisdom of the Acts of the Apostles: Saint Peter and the beggar, which reminds us that we can give only what we have (3:1–10); the tragic story of Ananias and Sapphira, who lied to the apostles and suffered the consequences (5:1–11); and Saint Peter and the baptism of Cornelius, the first Gentile Christian (chapter 10).

Concluding Prayer

Lord Jesus,
you entrusted your Church to the apostles.
Send your Holy Spirit upon their successors.
Let them hear your voice and obey you.
Draw us closer to you.
Help us to share your Good News.
Let us complete the mission you have given us.
Grant us your salvation.
Show us your glory.
For you are Lord forever and ever.
Amen.

Letters of Saint Paul

Romans
First Corinthians
Second Corinthians
Galatians
Ephesians
Philippians
Colossians
First Thessalonians
Second Thessalonians
First Timothy
Second Timothy
Titus
Philemon
Hebrews

Romans

Do not be conformed to this world but be transformed by the renewal of your mind, that you may prove what is the will of God, what is good and acceptable and perfect.

ROMANS 12:2

Opening Prayer
Lord Jesus,
you are all-holy
and righteous in all your ways.
You are just. You are good.
Send us your Spirit.
Convert our hearts.
Transform our minds.
Show us your glory.
For you are Lord forever and ever.
Amen.

Basic Message
Justification is available to all people in Jesus Christ. There is no partiality in the salvation offered to us by faith in the Lord Jesus.

Introductory Overview
In his Letter to the Romans, Saint Paul explains our salvation in Jesus Christ. The letter is a summary of the teachings he preached throughout his missionary efforts. He wanted to be sure that believers had sound doctrine. In his letter, he shows us

that humanity merits death because of sin, but we can receive salvation by faith in Jesus Christ. The apostle emphasizes that salvation is a free gift of God to those who believe. He further describes the way of life that those who believe should follow.

Basic Outline

The Letter to the Romans has six main parts:

- Chapter 1:1–17: Introduction.
- Chapters 1:18—4: Salvation is found in Jesus Christ alone.
- Chapters 5–8: An explanation of salvation.
- Chapters 9–11: Salvation is for all.
- Chapters 12—15:13: The way of life of those who believe.
- Chapters 15:14–16: Conclusion.

Application to Our Lives

In the Letter to the Romans 12:1–2, Saint Paul teaches that we need to allow for the renewal of our minds. We cannot think as the fallen world thinks. God's ways are not the ways of this world. We need to allow for a transformation of our minds so that we can know God's ways and be faithful to them.

In our lives, we have to be careful not to give too much power or influence to our thoughts or feelings. Simply because we think or feel something does not mean it's right. We have to discern our minds and hearts. We need a healthy suspicion of ourselves and should regularly examine our consciences and ask for the help of God's grace. Only in this way can we know the will of God and remain open to his ways.

Basic Points

Author: The Christian tradition attributes the Letter to the Romans to the apostle Paul. The letter is popularly hailed as the apostle's masterpiece. It is his most developed and esteemed letter.

Placement: The Letter to the Romans is the sixth book of the New Testament and the fifty-second book of the Bible.

Keywords:

- Righteousness: To be in a good relationship with God by believing in the Lord Jesus and living according to his way of life. This includes being faithful to the spiritual and moral demands of the Lord Jesus.
- Justification: The state of a soul that has been freed from sin and is now living in grace by the merits of Jesus Christ.
- Grace: The very life of God dwelling within a human soul.

Getting Started

While the eventual goal is to read all sixteen chapters of the Letter to the Romans, here are three selections that can get us started. Each selection shows us the depth and wisdom of the Letter to the Romans: the love the Lord Jesus has for us (8:31–37); the marks of a true Christian (12:9–21); and a warning not to judge others (14:1–12).

Concluding Prayer

Lord Jesus,
you gave us the great gift of our salvation.
Help us to live as your followers.
Transform our minds.

Strengthen our hearts.
Give us your grace.
Help us to be your witnesses.
Grant us your salvation.
For you are Lord forever and ever.
Amen.

First Corinthians

*Love is patient and kind; love is not jealous or boastful; it
is not arrogant or rude. Love does not insist on its own
way; it is not irritable or resentful; it does not rejoice at
wrong, but rejoices in the right. Love bears all things,
believes all things, hopes all things, endures all things.*

1 CORINTHIANS 13:4–7

Opening Prayer
Lord Jesus,
send us your Spirit.
Keep us safely under your care.
Remove all evil from our midst.
Protect us from division and false teaching.
For you are Lord forever and ever.
Amen.

Basic Message
As Christians, we are members of the Body of Christ and are
called to be united in him.

Introductory Overview
In his First Letter to the Corinthians, Saint Paul addresses some
false teachings and divisions that have developed in the Church
in Corinth. The apostle clarifies the teachings of the Lord Jesus
and calls the Corinthians to unity.

Basic Outline

The First Letter to the Corinthians has four main parts:

- Chapter 1:1–9: Introduction.
- Chapters 1:10—14: Moral questions and divisions within the community.
- Chapter 15: Clarification on the resurrection of the dead.
- Chapter 16: Conclusion.

Application to Our Lives

In his First Letter to the Corinthians, Saint Paul gives a beautiful description of love. He reminds us that love is to be patient and kind. In his summary, he casts out any spirits of selfishness or division. He calls us to love one another.

In our lives, we need to do a regular reboot on how we love. In our fallenness, it's easy to become envious, boastful, arrogant, or rude. We can quickly become irritable or resentful. We need to keep ourselves in check and regularly confess our sins. We need to desire to follow the way of the Lord and to love as he loves. If we are to love as Christ loves, we must ask for his help, battle our fallenness, and seek the strength and consolation of his grace.

Basic Points

Author: The Christian tradition attributes the First Letter to the Corinthians to the apostle Paul.

Placement: First Corinthians is the seventh book of the New Testament and the fifty-third book of the Bible. It is the first of two letters to the Church in Corinth.

Keywords:

- Corinth: A port city in southern Greece. During the time of the apostles, it was one of the largest cities in Greece. Saint Paul preached the Gospel there and formed a Christian community. Later, he wrote two letters to them.
- Unworthy manner: Saint Paul's teaching about reception of the Eucharist. He tells the Christians to be free from major sin when they eat the Lord's Body and drink the Lord's Blood. He warns them of condemnation if the Eucharist is received in an unworthy manner (see 11:17–34).
- One Body: The teaching of Saint Paul that every baptized Christian is a member of the Body of Christ and is united to every other believer. He uses the term to address division in the Church and calls everyone to a unity of belief and mission (see 12:12–31).
- "Most to be pitied": The term used by Saint Paul to describe Christians if the Resurrection didn't take place. They should be pitied by everyone because belief in the Resurrection is the heart of the Christian Faith (15:19). He uses the term to show how important it is for Christians to believe in the Resurrection.

Getting Started

While the eventual goal is to read all sixteen chapters of First Corinthians, here are three selections that can get us started. Each selection shows us the depth and wisdom of First Corinthians: God chooses the weak to accomplish great things (1:27–31); Saint Paul's call to unity (chapter 3); and the imperishable crown that awaits the faithful in heaven (9:24–25).

Concluding Prayer
Lord Jesus,
you are the Risen One.
You have destroyed sin and death.
You call us to yourself.
You summon us to love as you love.
You paid the price for our salvation.
Feed us with your Body and Blood.
Show us your glory.
For you are Lord forever and ever.
Amen.

Second Corinthians

And to keep me from being too elated by the abundance of revelations, a thorn was given me in the flesh, a messenger of Satan, to harass me, to keep me from being too elated. Three times I begged the Lord about this, that it should leave me; but he said to me, "My grace is sufficient for you, for my power is made perfect in weakness."

2 CORINTHIANS 12:7–9A

Opening Prayer

Lord Jesus,
we come before you, meek and humble of heart.
We acknowledge your sovereignty, your majesty, your glory.
We praise you. We love you.
Send us your Holy Spirit.
Give us the grace to do your will.
Help us to carry our cross.
Show us your glory.
For you are Lord forever and ever.
Amen.

Basic Message

God has a plan for each of us and calls us to a specific purpose. Those who are called to be apostles are a great blessing to the Church.

Introductory Overview

In his Second Letter to the Corinthians, Saint Paul responds to some harsh accusations against him and his ministry. Some were claiming that he was not a true apostle because he never saw the Lord Jesus before the Resurrection. They mocked his poverty and accused him of being an arrogant coward and a poor speaker. Saint Paul defends himself and his divinely direct call to be an apostle.

Basic Outline

The Second Letter to the Corinthians has five main parts:

- Chapter 1:1–14: Introduction.
- Chapters 1:15—7: Saint Paul defends himself and explains the apostolic ministry.
- Chapters 8–9: An appeal for generosity to the Church in Jerusalem.
- Chapters 10—13:10: Saint Paul defends his apostolic ministry.
- Chapter 13:11–14: Conclusion.

Application to Our Lives

In Second Corinthians, Saint Paul defends his apostolic ministry. In his explanation, he refers to many revelations and spiritual blessings he has received. He tempers this disclosure, however, by explaining the suffering that the Lord Jesus has allowed him to undergo. He tells us that he appealed to the Lord three times to have his suffering removed but that Jesus told him his grace was sufficient. Saint Paul accepted the Lord's will and offered up his sufferings, viewing them as a part of his vocation as an apostle.

In our lives, there are times when the Lord will allow us to suffer. We might also beg him three times to remove our sor-

rows or sufferings, and he might tell us that his grace is sufficient. Such moments can be distressing and upsetting, but they
can also be opportunities for us to declare our trust in and love
for the Lord. As the Lord Jesus carried his cross, so he calls us to
carry ours. There will be times — for our good or the good of
others, or both — when the Lord will permit sufferings in our
lives, including in the vocations he has given us. Our call is to
accept those sufferings, rely on his grace, and offer them up with
the Lord's own sufferings.

Basic Points
Author: The Christian tradition attributes the Second Letter to
the Corinthians to the apostle Paul.

Placement: Second Corinthians is the eighth book of the New
Testament and the fifty-fourth book of the Bible. It is the second
of two letters to the Church in Corinth.

Keywords:

- Apostolic ministry: The work and service of an apostle or his successors, who are called "bishops."
- Vocation: The call of a believer to a specific way of
  life or service in Jesus Christ.

Getting Started
While the eventual goal is to read all thirteen chapters of Second Corinthians, here are three selections that can get us started.
Each selection shows us the depth and wisdom of Second Corinthians: the consolations offered to us by God (1:3–5); walking by faith and not by sight (5:6–10); and our call to generosity
(9:6–11).

Concluding Prayer

Lord Jesus,
your grace is sufficient for us.
Help us to accept the sufferings of this world.
Guide us to know your will.
Strengthen us to fulfill our vocation.
Nourish us with your Body and Blood.
Show us your glory.
For you are Lord forever and ever.
Amen.

Galatians

*I have been crucified with Christ; it is no longer I
who live, but Christ who lives in me; and the life
I now live in the flesh I live by faith in the Son of
God, who loved me and gave himself for me.*

GALATIANS 2:20

Opening Prayer

Lord Jesus,
God of love,
we thank you for your saving mercy.
We bless you and praise you.
Help us to walk with you.
Keep our eyes fixed on your cross.
Strengthen us to suffer with you.
Teach us to love.
Grant us your salvation.
For you are Lord forever and ever.
Amen.

Basic Message

God offers us salvation in Jesus Christ. To accept this invitation, we must believe in Jesus Christ, be baptized, and follow his way of life. The distinctive laws and demands of the Old Covenant have been fulfilled and so are no longer required of God's people.

Introductory Overview

In his Letter to the Galatians, Saint Paul confronts and refutes false views being taught in different parts of Galatia. He emphasizes that the Old Testament laws and practices are no longer required of God's people. They have been fulfilled in Jesus Christ. He stresses that justification comes from Jesus Christ alone. In addition, Paul defends his apostolic ministry — which was being challenged in Galatia — and he also provides some autobiographical reflections.

Basic Outline

The Letter to the Galatians has five main parts:

- Chapter 1:1–10: Introduction.
- Chapters 1:11—2: Saint Paul defends his apostolic ministry.
- Chapters 3–4: Justification is found in Jesus Christ alone.
- Chapters 5—6:10: Freedom and love in Jesus Christ.
- Chapter 6:11–18: Conclusion.

Application to Our Lives

In Galatians 2:19–20, Saint Paul stresses the life we are called to live as disciples of Jesus Christ. We are called to die to ourselves, take up our crosses, and faithfully follow him along the way of love.

In our lives, we should rely on Jesus Christ and not search for any other religious customs, laws, or practices outside his New Covenant. We have Jesus Christ, and he is everything. As we live his way of love, the Lord gives us his sacraments; his mother, Mary; his Church; the Bible; his prayer; his holy ones, the saints; and all the other gifts of his New Covenant as ways in which his grace can be received and work within us. By accepting his grace, we become more of ourselves in him. Rather than allowing sin to take away the best parts of who we are, we let the power of grace cast out our sins and build up who we are called to be in Jesus Christ. In this way, we fully live only in Jesus Christ and by the workings of his grace. This is the reality that Saint Paul is describing. This is the reality offered to each of us.

Basic Points

Author: The Christian tradition attributes the Letter to the Galatians to the apostle Paul.

Placement: Galatians is the ninth book of the New Testament and the fifty-fifth book of the Bible.

Keywords:

- Galatia: An area in the highlands of modern-day central Turkey. At the time of the apostles, it was a Roman province. It was a region evangelized by Saint Paul in his missionary journeys.
- Judaizers: A group of Jewish Christians who believed it was necessary for all Christians, Jews, and Gentiles, to follow the distinctive laws and practices of the Old Covenant. Saint Paul responds to them and their false beliefs in his Letter to the Galatians.

Getting Started

While the eventual goal is to read all six chapters of Galatians, here are three selections that can get us started. Each selection shows us the depth and wisdom of the Letter to the Galatians: we are all one in Jesus Christ (3:23–29); the Spirit of adoption through which we call God "Abba" (4:1–7); and the fruits of

God's Spirit (5:22–26).

Concluding Prayer

Lord Jesus,
you are our Savior and Redeemer.
We turn to you alone.
We seek salvation in you alone.
Give us your grace.
Teach us your wisdom.
Help us to walk in your ways.
Show us your glory.
For you are Lord forever and ever.
Amen.

Ephesians

*I therefore, a prisoner for the Lord, beg you to walk
in a manner worthy of the calling to which you have
been called, with all lowliness and meekness, with
patience, forbearing one another in love, eager to
maintain the unity of the Spirit in the bond of peace.*

EPHESIANS 4:1–3

Opening Prayer

Lord Jesus,
God of love and truth,
you carry us from death to life.
You lead us from darkness to light.
Send us your Spirit.
Stir our hearts.
Defend us with your grace.
Grant us your salvation.
For you are Lord forever and ever.
Amen.

Basic Message

The Lord Jesus Christ has reconciled all humanity to the Father.
He is the head of the Church and the Lord of all creation.

Introductory Overview

In his Letter to the Ephesians, Saint Paul teaches that creation
is good, that Jesus Christ is the head of this creation and the

Church, and that his salvation is offered to all people. There is no secret or select group. There are no hidden ceremonies. There is no worship of angels. Various forms of these beliefs had entered the Ephesian community through the influence of the Greco-Roman culture. They each challenged the primacy of Jesus Christ over all creation. As such, Saint Paul emphasizes Christ as the first of all creation and the Savior who offers salvation to everyone. The apostle stresses the need for unity in the Church.

Basic Outline
The Letter to the Ephesians has four main parts:

- Chapter 1:1–2: Introduction.
- Chapters 1:3—3: The unity of all things in Jesus Christ.
- Chapters 4—6:20: The Christian way of life.
- Chapter 6:21–24: Conclusion.

Application to Our Lives
In his Letter to the Ephesians, Saint Paul is adamant about the supremacy and majesty of Jesus Christ. Jesus is the Lord of all things. Flowing from this central belief, Saint Paul deepens his teachings on how we are to live as disciples of the Lord Jesus, exhorting us to live in a manner worthy of the call we have received in Jesus Christ. As a help, Saint Paul develops the specifics of this call and describes the Christian way of life. We are to be humble, gentle, and patient, bearing with one another in love and seeking peace.

In our lives, we are called to die to our sinfulness, to take off our old selves, and to clothe ourselves in Jesus Christ. This takes many practical forms, such as showing humility when we are questioned about job performance; being gentle when someone cuts us off in traffic or is rude to us in the grocery store; being patient when someone interrupts us or when we have to wait in a line; bearing with someone who exhibits a harsh spirit; or laboring to keep peace with family members or friends who have been unkind or have offended us. In each of these ways, and in hundreds of others, we are called to put on the Lord Jesus and to follow his way of love. The Christian way is different from the way of the unbeliever. As Christians, we choose Jesus Christ and his way above all others.

Basic Points

Author: The Christian tradition attributes the Letter to the Ephesians to the apostle Paul.

Placement: Ephesians is the tenth book of the New Testament and the fifty-sixth book of the Bible. This is one of four letters Saint Paul wrote while in captivity.

Keywords:

- Ephesus: A city in west central modern-day Turkey. At the time of the apostles, it was a part of the Roman Empire. Saint Paul ministered in the city and spent a great deal of time with the early Christians there.
- Gnostic: A person who believes that a select group of people possesses secret knowledge. Gnostics tended to hate the material world, believing that only the spiritual world was good. Saint Paul discredits the Gnostics in his Letter to the Ephesians.

Getting Started

While the eventual goal is to read all six chapters of the Letter to the Ephesians, here are three selections that can get us started.

Each selection shows us the depth and wisdom of the Letter to the Ephesians: the plan of salvation in Jesus Christ (1:3–14; these verses may have been a song in the early Church); the old person giving way to a new person in Jesus Christ (4:25–32); and the spiritual battle of a disciple, including putting on the armor of God (6:10–20).

Concluding Prayer

Lord Jesus,
Lord of all creation,
Head of the Church,
save us.
Help us to follow your way.
Give us your grace.
Cover us with your protection.
Grant us the fruits of your Spirit.
Make us worthy of your salvation.
Show us your glory.
For you are Lord forever and ever.
Amen.

Philippians

Rejoice in the Lord always; again I will say, Rejoice.

PHILIPPIANS 4:4

Opening Prayer

Lord Jesus,
Son of the eternal Father,
you suffered and died for us.
We praise you. We thank you.
Help us to follow you.
Show us your way.
Grant us your salvation.
For you are Lord forever and ever.
Amen.

Basic Message

We are called to persevere in our faith, even when we are persecuted and when false teachers try to deceive us. We are called to imitate the Lord in his humility and obedience.

Introductory Overview

In his Letter to the Philippians, Saint Paul expresses his affection and gratitude for the faith of the Philippians. He also warns them against pride and vainglory, pointing to Christ as the model of humility. The apostle emphasizes salvation in Jesus Christ and denounces the influence and false teachings of the Judaizers.

Basic Outline

The Letter to the Philippians has five main parts:

- Chapter 1:1–26: Introduction and Paul's captivity.
- Chapters 1:27—2:18: Saint Paul calls for perseverance and points to Jesus Christ.
- Chapter 2:19–30: Updates on two companions of Saint Paul.
- Chapter 3: The correction of false teachings on justification.
- Chapter 4: Conclusion.

Application to Our Lives

In his Letter to the Philippians, Saint Paul speaks of the humility, sufferings, and obedience of Jesus Christ. The Lord's witness is used to encourage the Christians in Philippi in their own struggles. The apostle calls them to persevere and keep the faith. He even goes so far as to call them to rejoice in the midst of their hardships.

In our lives, when things become burdensome and we are tempted to let worry, anxiety, or fear take over our souls, Saint Paul recommends that we rejoice in the Lord. Difficult as life may sometimes be, we can rejoice because the Lord Jesus is with us and his grace is sufficient. He gives us the strength to endure whatever our fallen world gives us. So, rather than allowing distress and restlessness in our lives, we can take our problems and concerns to the Lord Jesus, knowing that he is with us and that we will triumph.

Basic Points

Author: The Christian tradition attributes the Letter to the Philippians to the apostle Paul.

Placement: Philippians is the eleventh book of the New Testament and the fifty-seventh book of the Bible. This is one of four letters Saint Paul wrote while in captivity.

Keywords:

- Philippi: A Roman colony and major port city in Macedonia (modern-day northeastern Greece) at the time of Saint Paul. The apostle established the Church there.

Getting Started

While the eventual goal is to read all four chapters of the Letter to the Philippians, here are three selections that can get us started. Each selection shows us the depth and wisdom of Philippians: the apostle's prayer for the Philippians and us (1:3–11); the call to imitate the Lord Jesus in his humility (2:5–11; these verses may have been a song in the early Church); and our goal of heaven (3:2–21).

Concluding Prayer

Lord Jesus,
you humbled yourself,
you clothed yourself in humility,
suffering and dying for us.
Help us to imitate you.
Give us your patience and humility.
Show us your way.
Let us rejoice in you always.
Grant us your salvation.
For you are Lord forever and ever.
Amen.

Colossians

And whatever you do, in word or deed, do everything in the name of the Lord Jesus, giving thanks to God the Father through him.

COLOSSIANS 3:17

Opening Prayer

Lord Jesus,
eternal Son of the Father,
firstborn of creation,
Lord of the angels,
head of the Church,
we glorify you!
We praise you. We exalt your name.
You are all-holy and ever-living.
Turn to us.
Grant us your salvation.
For you are Lord forever and ever.
Amen.

Basic Message

We must remain steadfast in our faith in Jesus Christ, through whom and in whom all creation was brought forth and continues to exist. We must worship God alone and be cautious of false teachings.

Introductory Overview

In his Letter to the Colossians, Saint Paul denounces false teachers who are causing a disturbance in the community. They are attempting to turn people away from the Lord Jesus in favor of a type of angel worship. Saint Paul encourages the Christian community to remain steadfast in their faith in Jesus.

Basic Outline

The Letter to the Colossians has four main parts:

- Chapter 1:1–14: Introduction.
- Chapters 1:15—3:4: The superiority of Christ and the danger of false teachers.
- Chapters 3:5—4:6: The way of life of believers.
- Chapter 4:7–18: Conclusion.

Application to Our Lives

In his Letter to the Colossians, Saint Paul reminds us that everything we do, we do for the Lord Jesus. No matter what our vocation, occupation, or work, we give or diminish our praise to the Lord by the degree of virtue, excellence, and hard work we put into our tasks. As disciples, we labor for the Lord.

In our lives, we need to realize that our work is for the Lord. It doesn't matter whether a boss is watching us, or colleagues see our excellence, or people recognize our accomplishments. Our labor and attentiveness to detail are given as an act of praise to the Lord Jesus. As such, we don't waste time, cut corners, cheat our employers, or compromise the quality of our work. We give everything to the Lord. We work hard, virtuously, and excellently for his praise.

Basic Points

Author: The Christian tradition attributes the Letter to the Colossians to the Apostle Paul. This is one of four letters Saint Paul wrote while in captivity. It is possible that Saint Paul never visited this city but wrote his letter as an apostolic intervention when he heard of the Colossians' false worship.

Placement: The Letter to the Colossians is the twelfth book of the New Testament and the fifty-eighth book of the Bible.

Keywords:

- Colossae: A city in the southwest corner of modern-day Turkey. At the time of the apostles, it was located along a major trade route through the Roman province of Asia Minor.
- Primacy of Christ: The conviction that Jesus Christ is superior to all created persons and things and that everything was created in and through him. Saint Paul asserts this belief in denouncing angel worship.
- Angel worship: The practice of idolatry that worshipped angels as gods. It was common in some spin-off groups of the Old Testament. Saint Paul argues against angel worship in his Letter to the Ephesians.

Getting Started

While the eventual goal is to read all four chapters of the Letter to the Colossians, here are three selections that can get us started. Each selection shows us the depth and wisdom of Colossians: the apostle's prayer (1:9–14); the fullness of life in Christ (2:8–14); and the Christian way of life (3:1–17).

Concluding Prayer

Lord Jesus,
you are the eternal Son of the Father;
you are the firstborn of all creation;
our very existence is your gift.
Help us to always look to you,
to seek your glory,
and to love you above all things.
Bless us with your grace.
Grant us your salvation.
For you are Lord forever and ever.
Amen.

First Thessalonians

*May the God of peace himself sanctify you wholly;
and may your spirit and soul and body be kept
sound and blameless at the coming of our Lord Jesus
Christ. He who calls you is faithful, and he will do it.*

1 THESSALONIANS 5:23–24

Opening Prayer

Lord Jesus,
you are ever-faithful.
You come to us in love.
In you, we live and move and have our being.
Help us to never turn away from you.
Grant us your strength.
Show us your glory.
For you are Lord forever and ever.
Amen.

Basic Message

We need to rely on the Lord Jesus when we're being persecuted. We need to follow his way of life and wait with joy for his Second Coming.

Introductory Overview

In his First Letter to the Thessalonians, Saint Paul encourages those who converted to the Lord Jesus by the apostolic preaching. Judaizers are actively persecuting and accusing new converts of heresy, yet many remain faithful. Saint Paul writes to the Thessalonians to reconnect with them and to inspire them to remain strong in the Lord.

Basic Outline

The First Letter to the Thessalonians has five main parts:

- Chapter 1:1: Introduction.
- Chapters 1:2—2:20: Saint Paul's response to the persecution of the Christians.
- Chapter 3: Timothy's mission from Saint Paul.
- Chapters 4–5:22: Waiting for the Second Coming and thus the fulfillment of the Christian way of life.
- Chapter 5:23–28: Conclusion.

Application to Our Lives

In First Thessalonians 5:23–24, Saint Paul reminds the early Christians of the Second Coming of the Lord Jesus. The perspective of eternity is an uplifting one because bad things happen — disasters occur, accidents strike, sickness hits, and persecutions befall us. When suffering comes, we tend to look inward or blame other people. Sometimes, there is accountability. But even in such moments, the full answers, solutions, and consolation we need cannot be found in the things of this world.

In our lives, we have to turn our hearts to the Lord Jesus, reminding ourselves about the fallenness of this world and that bad things happen even to good people. Still, it can be difficult for us to look beyond our own suffering. Many become paralyzed in pain, fear, denial, self-pity, or bitter anger. Saint Paul reminds us that our God is faithful. He is the God of peace. He is the God of our salvation, who constantly accompanies us and waits for us to share his joy fully in eternity. In difficult, disappointing, or disastrous moments, we can turn to him. We can remind ourselves that all these evils will pass and that one day we will be with the Lord Jesus forever in heaven.

Basic Points
Author: The Christian tradition attributes the First Letter to the Thessalonians to the apostle Paul.

Placement: First Thessalonians is the thirteenth book of the New Testament and the fifty-ninth book of the Bible. It is the first of two letters to the Thessalonians.

Keywords:

- Thessalonica: A port city on the Aegean Sea in Macedonia (modern-day Greece). The city was visited by Saint Paul, who preached and formed a Christian community there.
- Parousia: The Second Coming of Jesus Christ. It will mark the end of the world as we know it.

Getting Started
While the eventual goal is to read all five chapters of the First Letter to the Thessalonians, here are three selections that can get us started. Each selection shows us the depth and wisdom of First Thessalonians: the Second Coming of the Lord (4:13–18); our call to live as children of light (5:2–11); and an exhortation to Christian living (5:12–24).

Concluding Prayer
Lord Jesus,
you accepted persecution;
you did not avoid suffering.

Give us your strength.
Help us with your grace.
Strengthen us to fight the good fight.
Show us your glory.
For you are Lord forever and ever.
Amen.

Second Thessalonians

*Now concerning the coming of our Lord Jesus Christ and
our assembling to meet him, we beg you, brethren, not
to be quickly shaken in mind or excited, either by
spirit or by word, or by letter purporting to be from
us, to the effect that the day of the Lord has come.*

2 THESSALONIANS 2:1–2

Opening Prayer

Lord Jesus,
you fulfill our every hope;
you are our stronghold and our refuge.
Protect us against the pitfalls of this world.
Help us to follow your way.
Keep us faithful to you.
Grant us your salvation.
For you are Lord forever and ever.
Amen.

Basic Message

The Lord's Second Coming has not yet arrived. In the meantime,
Christians must persevere in living the way of the Lord Jesus.
When the Lord returns, there will be justice given to all.

Introductory Overview

In his Second Letter to the Thessalonians, Saint Paul addresses
the disciples' growing questions about the Lord's Second Com-

ing. The persecution against them has intensified, and they are fearful and bewildered about the return of the Lord. With this confusion, many people are refusing to work and are taking advantage of the generosity of other members of the community. Saint Paul addresses these matters and others in his second letter.

Basic Outline

The Second Letter to the Thessalonians has five main parts:

- Chapter 1:1–2: Introduction.
- Chapter 1:3–12: Gratitude for their perseverance in persecution.
- Chapter 2: The Second Coming and the man of lawlessness.
- Chapter 3:1–15: Prayer and work.
- Chapter 3:16–18: Conclusion.

Application to Our Lives

In his Second Letter to the Thessalonians, Saint Paul reminds the early Christians that the Lord Jesus will return in glory and judgment, but not yet. As they wait in joyful hope for his coming, they must remain virtuous, industrious, and hard-working. Saint Paul warns against those who claim to know when the Lord will return.

In our lives, we hear similar things, either about the return of the Lord or about the end of the earth. We must be ready, but we cannot allow fear to overtake us. Only love should motivate our hearts as we await the Second Coming. Rather than being drawn into needless anxiety or an empty restlessness, we need to take Saint Paul's advice. We are called to stand firm in the Lord Jesus, faithfully follow his way, and be focused on where the Lord has us today.

Basic Points

Author: The Christian tradition attributes the Second Letter to the Thessalonians to the apostle Paul.

Placement: Second Thessalonians is the fourteenth book of the New Testament and the sixtieth book of the Bible. It is the second of two letters to the Thessalonians.

Keywords:

- Man of lawlessness: Another term for the Antichrist, an especially nefarious opponent of Jesus Christ. He lies, causes confusion, and denies the divinity and saving power of the Lord.

Getting Started

While the eventual goal is to read all three chapters of the Second Letter to the Thessalonians, here are three selections that can get us started. Each selection shows us the depth and wisdom of Second Thessalonians: God's righteous judgment (1:5–12); our being chosen for salvation in Jesus Christ (2:13–17); and the summons to work hard (3:6–15).

Concluding Prayer

Lord Jesus,
we await your return with joyful hope.
Grant us your grace.
Help us to work hard.
Keep us strong and faithful.
Guide us in your way.
Grant us your salvation.
For you are Lord forever and ever.
Amen.

First Timothy

For the love of money is the root of all evils; it is through this craving that some have wandered away from the faith and pierced their hearts with many pangs.

1 TIMOTHY 6:10

Opening Prayer

Lord Jesus,
you are the one mediator between God and humanity.
All good things come from you.
Teach us your ways.
Guide our leaders.
Send them your Holy Spirit.
Help us to be humble and obedient.
Grant us your salvation.
For you are Lord forever and ever.
Amen.

Basic Message

Pastoral leadership comes to us from God. It is grounded in the apostolic ministry and is focused on guarding and protecting the Gospel and helping us receive salvation in Jesus Christ.

Introductory Overview

In his First Letter to Timothy, Saint Paul gives guidance and encouragement to Saint Timothy, the young bishop of Ephesus. Timothy was from the city of Lystra, where he met Saint Paul, the man who became his spiritual father and mentor for many years. Over time, Saint Paul began sending Timothy on missions to different churches, and he eventually appointed Timothy to serve as a bishop. Throughout this letter, Saint Paul instructs Saint Timothy on effective pastoral care, such as taking charge of a community and addressing issues related to false teachings.

Basic Outline
The First Letter to Timothy has four main parts:

- Chapter 1:1–2: Introduction.
- Chapters 1:3—4:11: False teachers and good discipline.
- Chapters 4:12—6:2: Fatherly counsel from Saint Paul to Saint Timothy.
- Chapter 6:3–21: Conclusion.

Application to Our Lives
In his First Letter to Timothy, Saint Paul addresses many areas of pastoral leadership and the Christian way of life. In particular, in 1 Timothy 6:3–10, the apostle warns against greed and calls for a rightly ordered use of money. He teaches us that the love of money is the root of all kinds of evil.

In our lives, we all want to be comfortable, to pay our bills, and to have nice things. But there is a point when material things begin to take priority over virtuous or spiritual things. We begin to want more. We overspend and live beyond our means. We work more than necessary to cover expenses. We neglect our spiritual duties, family, and community involvement. We neglect the poor and others in need. We become greedy. We forget that we have money in order to live; we do *not* live to make money. Living to make money is a sad and dangerous downward spiral. As Christians, we are called to break free from it. We spend what we have. We pay our bills. We discipline our wants. We confess our jealousy of other people's prosperity. We serve the poor and those in need. We express heartfelt gratitude for what God has given to us. We rejoice!

Basic Points

Author: The Christian tradition attributes the First Letter to Timothy to the apostle Paul.

Placement: First Timothy is the fifteenth book of the New Testament and the sixty-first book of the Bible. It is the first of three pastoral letters written by Saint Paul.

Keywords:

- Bishop: A successor of the apostles. As a sign of deference to the original apostles, the term *bishop*, rather than apostle, was used for leadership after the apostolic age. Only the actual apostles would bear the title *apostle*. Each bishop, however, carries on the mission of the apostles. Saint Timothy was a bishop.
- Seared conscience: A conscience that has been gravely impaired by sin. A person with such a conscience is very resistant to feeling any guilt or remorse for his sinful actions (see 4:1–4).

Getting Started

While the eventual goal is to read all six chapters of the First Letter to Timothy, here are three selections that can get us started. Each selection shows us the depth and wisdom of First Timothy: our call to prayer (2:1–6); "the mystery of faith," which is an expression used in the Eucharistic Prayer at Mass (3:14–16); and a good minister of Jesus Christ (4:6–10).

Concluding Prayer

Lord Jesus,
Savior and Mediator,
you are the King of the ages,
immortal, invisible, the only true God.
To you be the glory, honor, and power forever.
Heal our wounds. Strengthen your Church.
Fill us with your Holy Spirit.
Keep us close to you.
Grant us your salvation.
Show us your glory.
For you are Lord forever and ever.
Amen.

Second Timothy

*And the Lord's servant must not be quarrelsome
but kindly to every one, an apt teacher,
forbearing, correcting his opponents with gentleness.*

2 TIMOTHY 2:24–25A

Opening Prayer

Lord Jesus,
you are the Light of the world.
We seek the help of your grace.
Free us from idolatry.
Direct our hearts to you.
Fill us with your hope.
Grant us your salvation.
For you are Lord forever and ever.
Amen.

Basic Message

We must believe, live, and teach according to the Apostolic Tradition and give strong opposition to any false and corrupt teachers.

Introductory Overview

In his Second Letter to Timothy, Saint Paul writes from prison in Rome. This is likely his last letter and the most personal of all his letters. He is writing to a spiritual son, knowing that his own life is coming to an end. In many respects, therefore, the letter is Saint Paul's last will and testament. It is an encouragement and an exhortation to Timothy to continue his apostolic mission with strength, courage, and vigor.

Basic Outline
The Second Letter to Timothy has four main parts:

- Chapter 1:1–2: Introduction.
- Chapters 1:3—2:13: Gratitude and pastoral instructions.
- Chapters 2:14—4:8: Fidelity to right teaching and false teachers.
- Chapter 4:9–22: Conclusion.

Application to Our Lives
In his Second Letter to Timothy, Saint Paul highlights the importance of kindness, patience, and gentleness, especially when teaching or correcting others. This was wisdom in the early Church, and it is wisdom today. As believers, we can be right and wrong at the same time, meaning we can be right in what we say but completely wrong in how we say it. We can teach or share the Gospel in a spirit that is foreign to the Gospel itself. We are called to follow the Lord's path of love, to seek civility and friendship with others, and to be kind in expressing the Gospel, our thoughts, and our opinions. We also must respect our neighbor and listen patiently to the words of others, especially when they disagree with us.

In our world today, we need this warning about not being quarrelsome. Our society has become very entrenched in specific views and a widespread spirit of unkindness and harshness to those who might disagree with a specific side or policy. Civility struggles to be shown and has been dethroned in many areas by partisan hostility and dismissiveness. We are called to be different. We must listen to Paul's admonitions and seek to be faithful to the

Lord's own way. When others do not listen, we listen more. When others are unkind, we go the extra mile in courtesy. When others demonize a neighbor, we seek to find the good in that person. In all things, we choose Christ and his most excellent way of love.

Basic Points

Author: The Christian tradition attributes the Second Letter to Timothy to the apostle Paul.

Placement: Second Timothy is the sixteenth book of the New Testament and the sixty-second book of the Bible. It is the second of three pastoral letters written by Saint Paul.

Keywords:

- Apostolic Tradition: The teachings and way of life of the Lord Jesus that were given to the apostles and passed down from them through every generation by the power of the Holy Spirit.
- Paul's captivity: Saint Paul was held in captivity in Rome. As a Roman citizen, he appealed to the Roman emperor and was awaiting a decision. The apostle knew the verdict would be against him and prepared to die for the Gospel. He was later beheaded for the Faith.

Getting Started

While the eventual goal is to read all four chapters of the Second Letter to Timothy, here are three selections that can get us started. Each selection shows us the depth and wisdom of Second Timothy: Saint Paul's encouragement never to be ashamed of the Gospel (1:8–14); the importance of the Sacred Scriptures (3:16–17); and a summons to faithfulness (4:1–5).

Concluding Prayer

Lord Jesus,
you are the way and the truth and the life.
We seek your face. We follow you alone.
Inspire our minds. Strengthen our hearts.
Help us to be kind, patient, and gentle.
Give us your grace.
Grant us your salvation.
For you are Lord forever and ever.
Amen.

Titus

Show yourself in all respects a model of good deeds,
and in your teaching show integrity, gravity, and sound
speech that cannot be censured, so that an opponent
may be put to shame, having nothing evil to say of us.

TITUS 2:7–8

Opening Prayer

Lord Jesus,
you have shown us the way to the Father.
Keep us faithful to your teachings.
Help us to live your way of love.
Guide our efforts to share your Gospel.
Strengthen us. Convict us.
Show us your presence.
For you are Lord forever and ever.
Amen.

Basic Message

We must teach what the apostles handed down to us and live virtuous lives worthy of our call in Jesus Christ.

Introductory Overview

In his Letter to Titus, Saint Paul instructs Titus, a Gentile Christian and the young bishop of Crete. The culture of Crete was well known in the ancient world, with the name *Cretan* a synonym for liar. Cretans had the reputation of being a violent and greedy people, and their cities were filled with corruption. Saint Paul had evangelized parts of the island and established the Church there. He appointed Titus, a spiritual son, to be its bishop. It fell to Titus, therefore, to call the Christians of Crete to remain steadfast in following the Way of the Lord Jesus. The apostle's letter is meant to serve as an encouragement to Titus in his difficult mission.

Basic Outline
The Letter to Titus has four main parts:

- Chapter 1:1–4: Introduction.
- Chapter 1:5–16: Good and bad leadership.
- Chapters 2—3:11: The Christian way of life.
- Chapter 3:12–15: Conclusion.

Application to Our Lives
In his Letter to Titus, Saint Paul reminds us that our witness must be both a virtuous life and well-spoken words. We cannot speak about a message we do not live, and we cannot speak poorly of the great gift we have received in Jesus Christ. The task of the disciple, and of Church leadership, is to be a strong witness to the Lord in every way.

In our lives, Saint Paul makes clear, we must model the Faith we share. If not, we will lose credibility with the world around us and thus diminish the likelihood that someone will accept the Gospel. And so, we have to work on our own discipleship. We also have to study and be ready to explain the Gospel well to those who might ask us about it. Of course, we are fallen, but we must continually seek to do our best for the Lord Jesus.

Basic Points
Author: The Christian tradition attributes the Letter to Titus to

the apostle Paul.

Placement: Titus is the seventeenth book of the New Testament and the sixty-third book of the Bible. It is the third of three pastoral letters written by Saint Paul.

Keywords:

- Crete: An island in the Mediterranean Sea that Saint Paul evangelized. The culture of Crete was at odds with the Christian way of life. Saint Paul appointed Saint Titus as its bishop.

Getting Started
While the eventual goal is to read all three chapters of the Letter to Titus, here are three selections that can get us started. Each selection shows us the depth and wisdom of Titus: the duty of leadership (1:7–9); our hope as Christians (2:11–13); and the Christian way of life (3:1–11).

Concluding Prayer
Lord Jesus,
you gave us the gift of our salvation.
You are love and mercy.
Help us to follow you.
Guide us to share the Gospel with others.
Grant us your grace.
Show us your glory.
For you are Lord forever and ever.
Amen.

Philemon

Accordingly, though I am bold enough in Christ to command you to do what is required, yet for love's sake I prefer to appeal to you.

<small>PHILEMON 8–9A</small>

Opening Prayer

Lord Jesus,
out of pure and abundant love,
you called us out of darkness.
You brought us into your own wonderful light.
We turn to you. We seek your grace.
Help us to follow you.
Grant us your salvation.
For you are Lord forever and ever.
Amen.

Basic Message

We are called to love one another as brothers and sisters in Jesus Christ.

Introductory Overview

In his Letter to Philemon, Saint Paul addresses Philemon, a wealthy member of the Colossian Church whose slave Onesimus escaped and ran away. Onesimus went to Rome, where he met with Saint Paul in captivity and embraced the Gospel. Although Saint Paul wants to keep Onesimus with him, he is required by Roman law to send him back. So Saint Paul sends Onesimus back to Philemon with a letter. In the letter, he asks Philemon to accept his former slave as a true brother in Christ.

Philemon contains only one chapter, so citations from Philemon include only the verses. For example, "Philemon 8" means Philemon, chapter 1, verse 8.

Basic Outline

The Book of Philemon consists of four main parts within a single chapter:

- Verses 1–3: Introduction.
- Verses 4–7: Praise of Philemon's love and faith.
- Verses 8–21: An appeal that Onesimus be welcomed back as a brother.
- Verses 22–25: Conclusion.

Application to Our Lives

In his Letter to Philemon, Saint Paul calls Philemon to do the right thing. As an apostle, he could command the disciple to obey him on this matter of justice. However, Saint Paul understands fallen human nature and its rebelliousness. He does not want to provoke Philemon. He instead appeals to the man's faith and exhorts him to consider his new spiritual brotherhood in Christ with Onesimus. As the apostle knows our fallenness, he also knows our goodness and the power of God's grace. As he desires Philemon to choose freely what is right and just, so he calls us to do the same today.

In our lives, we must open our hearts to the Gospel summons and do the right thing. We shouldn't need the weight of apostolic authority to command us. We should willingly listen to and obey what the Gospel asks of us, no matter how hard or culturally unpopular it is. In a similar way, when guiding others to know and do what is right, we would do well to remember Saint Paul's pastoral example: It is better to move people's consciences than to command their hearts.

Basic Points
Author: The Christian tradition attributes the Letter to Philemon to the apostle Paul.

Placement: Philemon is the eighteenth book of the New Testament and the sixty-fourth book of the Bible. This is one of four letters Saint Paul wrote while in captivity.

Keywords:

- Slavery: The ownership of one person by another. The practice is evil. It took the early Church some time to convert the hearts of believers to accept this teaching.
- Spiritual siblings: The spiritual reality that Christians are true brothers and sisters in Jesus Christ. Saint Paul emphasizes this lesson to Philemon.

Getting Started
The Letter to Philemon is one chapter of twenty-five verses. It is an easy read in one sitting. As a help, here are three verses to encourage us: Saint Paul's spiritual fatherhood (10); our relation to one another as siblings (15–16); and our summons to obedience (21).

Concluding Prayer
Lord Jesus,
you did everything out of love.
You ransomed us.

You have given us our freedom.
You call us to imitate you.
Show us your way.
Strengthen us with your grace.
Help us to trust and obey your will.
Grant us your salvation.
For you are Lord forever and ever.
Amen.

Hebrews

And let us consider how to stir up one another to love and good works, not neglecting to meet together, as is the habit of some, but encouraging one another, and all the more as you see the Day drawing near.

HEBREWS 10:24–25

Opening Prayer

Lord Jesus,
God of love and mercy,
Lord of the angels,
Head of your Church,
eternal Sacrifice of our salvation,
we worship you. We praise you.
Come to us.
Help us with your grace.
Strengthen us to persevere.
Show us your glory.
For you are Lord forever and ever.
Amen.

Basic Message

We must remain faithful to Jesus Christ, who is superior to the angels and the Old Testament holy ones. Despite persecution, we must persevere in our faith and seek the reward of heaven.

Introductory Overview

The Letter to the Hebrews was written to a Jewish-Christian community. It is possible that the letter was originally a homily preached in the early Church. Although it is unknown where the community was located, it is evident within the letter that they were facing persecution and imprisonment as followers of Jesus Christ. As a result, some were abandoning their faith in Jesus. The letter encourages them to persevere in their faith and restore their zeal for the Gospel.

Basic Outline

The Letter to the Hebrews has four main parts:

- Chapters 1–2: Jesus Christ is superior to the angels.
- Chapters 3–10: Jesus Christ as high priest and superior to all the Old Testament holy ones.
- Chapters 11–12: The praise of Old Testament holy ones and a warning against refusing the grace of God.
- Chapter 13: Conclusion.

Application to Our Lives

In the Letter to the Hebrews, the author reminds us about the demands of the Christian life. In particular, we are told in Hebrews 10:24–25 how important it is to meet together regularly. Placed within the context of the entire letter — which is all about formal worship — and within a broader historical context, this admonition most likely references the Church and her worship. The author is stressing the importance of gathering as believers and participating in the formal worship of the Church.

In our lives as believers, worship is the highest praise we can give to God. As members of the baptized, we are called to be present at the Eucharist and to receive Holy Communion in a worthy manner. The Church teaches us that such worship is "the source and summit" of our entire lives. It is the most important thing we do all week. As such, we need to make it a priority. We need to give ourselves time to recollect and prepare for the Eucharistic Sacrifice. We can't let anything take us away from worship. We can't allow ourselves to be distracted. As Christians, we are called to meet together. We are called to be at Mass.

Basic Points

Author: The Christian tradition attributes the Letter to the Hebrews to the apostle Paul, although a Jewish Christian disciple of the apostle — who was well versed in the ceremonies and liturgies of the Old Testament — likely may have written it.

Placement: Hebrews is the nineteenth book of the New Testament and the sixty-fifth book of the Bible.

Keywords:

- Meet together: A term used in the Letter to the Hebrews to reference public worship. The public worship of the Christians has been called by many names, such as the Breaking of the Bread, the Eucharist, and the Mass.
- High Priest: The esteemed leader of worship in the Temple. The Lord Jesus is identified as the perfect High Priest forever (see chapter 8).
- Melchizedek: A priest of the Most High God early in salvation history. The Lord Jesus held the same priesthood as Melchizedek. It was a new priesthood that fulfilled and completed the former priestly class of Aaron and the Levites (see Gn 14:18–20; Heb 7).
- Apostasy: The formal abandonment of belief in Jesus Christ.

Getting Started

While the eventual goal is to read all thirteen chapters of the Letter to the Hebrews, here are three selections that can get us started. Each selection shows us the depth and wisdom of Hebrews: the power of the word of God (4:12–13); the sacrifice of Jesus Christ (9:11–14); and an encouragement to persevere (10:19–25).

Concluding Prayer

Lord Jesus,
eternal High Priest,
everlasting Sacrifice,
you bless us with salvation.
We praise and adore you!
We glorify the wonders of your love!
We come and meet together.
We worship you. We exalt you.
Help us to love you.
Keep us steadfast.
Show us your glory.
For you are Lord forever and ever.
Amen.

Universal Letters

James
First Peter
Second Peter
First John
Second John
Third John
Jude

James

So the tongue is a little member and boasts of great things.

JAMES 3:5

Opening Prayer
Lord Jesus,
Protector of the poor,
Guardian of the vulnerable,
help us to imitate you.
We desire to continue your work.
Help us to love all people.
Turn our hearts to those in need.
Bless our faith. Strengthen our hope.
Show us your glory.
For you are Lord forever and ever.
Amen.

Basic Message
As Christians, we are called to live out our faith in Jesus Christ by words and deeds.

Introductory Overview
The Letter of James is addressed to the "twelve tribes in the Dispersion" (Jas 1:1), which is a symbolic way of saying the Jewish Christians who were outside the Promised Land. As such, it is addressed not to a specific community but to a universal group of people. Relying heavily on the wisdom books of the Old Tes-

tament and the Lord's Sermon on the Mount, James calls for an integrated faith in the hearts of believers. In twelve counsels, he reminds believers of the demands of Christian discipleship and calls on them to do good and avoid evil.

Basic Outline
The Letter of James has two main parts, and there is no conclusion to the letter:

- Chapter 1: Introduction.
- Chapters 2–5: Twelve counsels on the Christian way of life.

Application to Our Lives
In James 3:1–12, the apostle reminds us of the power of our tongues and of our spoken words. He warns us to be cautious about our tongues. While the tongue is a small member of the body, it's an effective and instrumental one. It can move and shape our lives. We need to be attentive and virtuous in how we use our tongues in speaking to and about other people.

We should use our tongues to praise God and build up those around us. We should avoid slander, gossip, and blasphemy of every kind. We should speak words of kindness and tenderness. If we must correct or admonish, our words should exude compassion and understanding. As Christians, we accept such wisdom as applicable toward all, but especially toward those who frustrate us, are unkind to us, or provoke our sense of virtue. Such people should be given even greater words of warmth and goodwill.

Basic Points
Author: The Christian tradition attributes the Letter of James to the kinsman of the Lord Jesus, James the first bishop of Jerusalem.

Placement: James is the twentieth book of the New Testament and the sixty-sixth book of the Bible.

Keywords:

- Dispersion: The Jewish Christians who were not living in the Promised Land (see 1:1).
- Kinsman: A family member. Saint James is identified as a kinsman of the Lord Jesus. Such a title could mean cousin or half-brother.
- Faith and works: The combined dynamics that are required for salvation in Jesus Christ (see 2:14–26).

Getting Started

While the eventual goal is to read all five chapters of the Letter of James, here are three selections that can get us started. Each selection shows us the depth and wisdom of the Letter of James: trial and temptation (1:12–18); a warning against partiality (2:1–13); and a warning to rich oppressors (5:1–6).

Concluding Prayer

Lord Jesus,
you call us to yourself.
You unite what is scattered.
Help us to hear your voice.
Show us your way.
Teach us your wisdom.
Let us serve you in others,
especially the weak and the vulnerable.
Grant us your salvation. Show us your glory.
For you are Lord forever and ever.
Amen.

First Peter

Cast all your anxieties on him, for he cares about you.

1 PETER 5:7

Opening Prayer

Lord Jesus,
chief Shepherd of all,
direct and guide us along your way.
Correct our faults.
Strengthen our weaknesses.
Help us to persevere.
We trust in you. We praise you.
For you are Lord forever and ever.
Amen.

Basic Message

As Christians, we are summoned to live holy and virtuous lives as we await our salvation in Jesus Christ. We must be willing to accept sufferings and persecutions for our faith in the Lord.

Introductory Overview

In the First Letter of Peter, the apostle addresses Christians in Asia Minor, who are undergoing persecution for their faith in Jesus Christ. The recipients of the letter are both Jewish Christians and Gentile Christians. In the letter, however, Saint Peter applies language and events in salvation history to both groups, indicating that every Christian is an heir to the work of God in the Old Testament. The apostle encourages them to understand the great gift of salvation they have received in Jesus and so live virtuous lives, including being ready to suffer persecution out of love for Christ.

Basic Outline
The First Letter of Peter has four main parts:

- Chapter 1:1–12: Introduction.
- Chapters 1:13—4:11: The call to holiness.
- Chapters 4:12—5:11: Counsel for times of persecution.
- Chapter 5:12–14: Conclusion.

Application to Our Lives
In the First Letter of Peter, the apostle seeks to encourage and inspire Christians persecuted for their faith in Jesus Christ. In 1 Peter 5, he calls the elders (and the entire community) to accept sufferings in living holy lives. In his counsel, he tells them to surrender their anxieties and worries to the Lord, who cares for them.

For our own lives, the chief apostle of the Lord Jesus provides us with similar wisdom. As we worry about loved ones, finances, health, work, and all the other things of our world, we can become frenzied in our stress and lose our peace. In response, Peter reminds us how much Jesus loves us, including how he desires to bless us in various ways. We need to turn to the Lord, give him our anxiety, ask for his grace, accept his strength, and then do our best in the midst of the trials of this world.

Basic Points
Author: The Christian tradition attributes the First Letter of Peter to Peter of Capernaum, the chief apostle of the Lord Jesus and our first pope.

Placement: First Peter is the twenty-first book of the New Testament and the sixty-seventh book of the Bible. It is the first of two letters written by Saint Peter.

Keywords:

- Pope: Literally meaning "father," it is the title given to the chief apostle of the Church. Saint Peter was the first pope. There have been 266 popes from Saint Peter to Pope Francis.
- Asia Minor: The western extremity of Asia and roughly equivalent to the Asian part of modern-day Turkey. At the time of the apostles, it was a Roman province.
- Harrowing of hell: The descent of the Lord Jesus' human soul into "hell" after his death on the cross but before his resurrection. On this occasion, the Lord welcomed all the holy ones of the Old Testament into heaven. They had been waiting for the coming of the Anointed Savior and could not enter paradise without him. Saint Peter alludes to this mysterious event (see 3:18–20), which is also referenced in the Apostles' Creed.
- Hell: Originally, the term meant a holding cell. Later it became associated with the place of the damned. In the First Letter of Peter and in the Apostles' Creed, it refers to a holding cell for the holy ones who died before Jesus Christ.
- Silvanus: One of the scribes of Saint Peter. He assisted in the writing of the apostle's first letter (see 5:12).

Getting Started

While the eventual goal is to read all five chapters of the First Letter of Peter, here are three selections that can get us started. Each selection shows us the depth and wisdom of the First Letter of Peter: the apostle's call to holiness (1:13–25); suffering as a Christian (4:12–19); and words of counsel to Church leaders (5:1–11).

Concluding Prayer

Lord Jesus,
eternal God and Shepherd of your people,
we choose you.
We follow you. We adore you.
We will suffer for you.
You are the Suffering Servant and mighty God.
We desire to be with you.
Call us to yourself.
Grant us your strength.
Show us your glory.
For you are Lord forever and ever.
Amen.

Second Peter

They promise them freedom, but they
themselves are slaves of corruption; for whatever
overcomes a man, to that he is enslaved.

2 PETER 2:19

Opening Prayer
Lord Jesus,
God and Savior,
come to us.
We await your return with joyful hope.
Help us to be ready.
Clothe us in holiness.
Grant us your grace.
We wait for you!
For you are Lord forever and ever.
Amen.

Basic Message
The Lord Jesus will one day return to us in glory. It will occur at a time we do not know, and we must be ready by living a holy life. We must avoid false teachers.

Introductory Overview
In the Second Letter of Peter, the apostle addresses concerns over the Lord's Second Coming. Many thought the Lord Jesus would return in their lifetimes and were confused because he

hadn't yet returned. Saint Peter reminds believers that the Lord will return on his schedule. In our response today, we must be ready by seeking lives of holiness. The apostle also warns against preachers who give false teachings about the Lord's return. It's possible that the letter may have originally been a homily in the early Church.

Basic Outline
The Second Letter of Peter has five main parts:

- Chapter 1:1–2: Introduction.
- Chapter 1:3–21: A call to holiness.
- Chapter 2: The punishment of false teachers.
- Chapter 3:1–16: The Lord's delay and the Second Coming.
- Chapter 3:17–18: Conclusion.

Application to Our Lives
In Second Peter 2, the apostle unmasks the influence and deception of false teachers. Freedom is the power to do what is right and noble. In Jesus Christ, we have freedom. False teachers promise freedom but only enslave those who listen to them. Our fallen nature is weak. It is prone to the slavery of sin. Our freedom rests on the grace God gives us through Jesus Christ.

In our lives, there are many false teachers. We are told, among other things, to obey our thirst, that love is love, and that we should have things our way right away. These are selfish tendencies that can lead us into moral and spiritual slavery. False teachers abound. We need to be attentive to what goes into our minds and hearts. We need to be discerning about our entertainment, the influence of marketing, the push of social media, and the slogans of our culture, avoiding sinful messaging and searching for good and uplifting things. We were made by and for God. We are called to freedom and to live in the joy of God's truth and holiness. And so we need to avoid false teachers and seek out those who will encourage and affirm authentic goodness in our lives.

Basic Points

Author: The Christian tradition attributes the Second Letter of Peter to Peter of Capernaum, the chief apostle of the Lord Jesus.

Placement: Second Peter is the twenty-second book of the New Testament and the sixty-eighth book of the Bible. It is the second of two letters written by Saint Peter.

Keywords:

- Divine Nature: The life of God and the attributes associated with him. Saint Peter teaches that through Jesus Christ, we will share in the Divine Nature (see 1:3–4).

Getting Started

While the eventual goal is to read all three chapters of the Second Letter of Peter, here are three selections that can get us started. Each selection shows us the depth and wisdom of Second Peter: the apostle's reminder of our salvation in Jesus Christ (1:3–15); the apostle recounts the Lord's Transfiguration (1:16–19); and the Lord Jesus delays his return so that more might be saved (3:8–10).

Concluding Prayer

Lord Jesus,
everlasting God,
to you one day

is like a thousand years,
and a thousand years like one day.
We long for you.
We await your glorious return.
Help us to be ready.
Make us holy.
Keep us strong.
Grant us your grace.
Show us your glory.
For you are Lord forever and ever.
Amen.

First John

If any one says, "I love God," and hates his brother, he is a liar; for he who does not love his brother whom he has seen, cannot love God whom he has not seen.

1 JOHN 4:20

Opening Prayer

Lord Jesus,
your love has saved us.
We thank and praise you.
Forgive our sins.
Grant us your grace.
Help us to learn from you.
Strengthen us to love one another.
Show us your glory.
For you are Lord forever and ever.
Amen.

Basic Message

God is love. As Christians, we must abide in him and love one another. We must avoid false teachers.

Introductory Overview

In the First Letter of John, the apostle encourages believers to remain faithful. He reminds us of the demands of discipleship and calls us to reject false teachings.

Basic Outline

The First Letter of John has four main parts:

- Chapter 1:1–4: Introduction.
- Chapters 1:5—4:6: Living as God's children.
- Chapters 4:7—5:12: Faith and love.
- Chapter 5:13–21: Conclusion.

Application to Our Lives

In First John 4, Saint John teaches us that God is love. Those who abide in love abide in God, and God abides in them. The apostle teaches us that perfect love casts out fear, so there is no fear in love. John also teaches us that God loved us first, which is how we can love him and our neighbor. The two dimensions of our love — God and neighbor — go together. And so we are warned about those who claim to love God but hate their brothers and sisters. Such people are liars and false teachers.

In our lives, we are called to love those around us — yes, even the ones who annoy us and frustrate us, including those who have bad breath, eat with their mouths open, or cause us discomfort. It's easy for us to make the broad statement "I love my neighbor," but then our neighbors come face to face with us, things become very specific, and we begin to dislike them. It's in these moments that God invites us to truly love another person. Love is seeing more than just what perturbs us. It's seeing another child of God and that person's dignity. It's dying to our own preferences and dislikes and showing others acceptance and kindness. The degree to which we can do this for our neighbor is the degree to which we truly love God.

Basic Points

Author: The Christian tradition attributes the First Letter of John to the apostle John, brother of James and son of Zebedee.

Placement: First John is the twenty-third book of the New Testament and the sixty-ninth book of the Bible. It is the first of three letters written by Saint John.

Keywords:

- Antichrist: Any false teacher who denies that Jesus is God and the Anointed Savior.
- In the flesh: The term used to describe the Lord Jesus, who is true God and true man. Many false teachers denied that the Lord Jesus was a real man with a true body. This was a Gnostic tendency that found its way into some communities in the early Church. Saint John strongly denounces this false teaching.

Getting Started
While the eventual goal is to read all five chapters of the First Letter of John, here are three selections that can get us started. Each selection shows us the depth and wisdom of First John: God is light (1:5–10); our call to obedience (2:1–6); and God is love (4:7–21).

Concluding Prayer
Lord Jesus,
Righteous One,
true God and true man,
save us!
Come to our aid.
Show us your love.
Teach us obedience.
Help us to love.
Show us your glory.
For you are Lord forever and ever.
Amen.

Second John

And this is love, that we follow his commandments;
this is the commandment, as you have heard
from the beginning, that you follow love.

2 JOHN 6

Opening Prayer
Lord Jesus,
you are merciful and just.
You have blessed us with your commandments.
Grant us your grace.
Help us to follow your way.
Keep us faithful.
We love you. We desire to serve you.
Show us your glory.
For you are Lord forever and ever.
Amen.

Basic Message
We must stay true to our faith in Jesus Christ, true God and true man, by following his commandments and avoiding false teachers.

Introductory Overview
In the Second Letter of John, the apostle addresses "the elect lady and her children" (verse 1). This is most likely a local community of the Church, since the feminine is often used in

speaking of the Church. The apostle calls believers to faithfulness and obedience to the Gospel and its moral demands. He thus warns us to avoid false teachers who deny the humanity of the Lord Jesus.

Second John contains only one chapter, so citations from Second John include only the verses. For example, "2 John 6" means Second John, chapter 1, verse 6.

Basic Outline

The Second Letter of John consists of four main parts within a single chapter:

- Verses 1–3: Introduction.
- Verses 4–6: Faithfulness and the call to love.
- Verses 7–12: Warning against antichrists.
- Verse 13: Conclusion.

Application to Our Lives

In the Second Letter of John, the apostle notes that many deceivers have gone out into the world. In spite of them, we are called to remain faithful. In Second John 6, the apostle reminds us that love involves keeping the commandments. Today, there are also many opinions about who Jesus is, diverse critiques of the Christian Faith, and arguments over the spiritual and moral claims made by the Lord Jesus and his Church. In this arena, it's easy to fall into doubt, question what is true, and feel spiritually bewildered.

In our lives, however, we are called to be firmly anchored in our faith, to know with certainty that Jesus Christ is God and Savior, and to obey his commandments and remain faithful to his way of love. We look to the teaching of the Church for this certitude. Despite dissenting opinions, including from the false teachers among us, we are called to walk with the Lord.

Basic Points

Author: The Christian tradition attributes the Second Letter of John to the apostle John, brother of James and son of Zebedee.

Placement: Second John is the twenty-fourth book of the New Testament and the seventieth book of the Bible. It is the second of three letters written by Saint John.

Keywords:

- Mother Church: A title of affection given to the Body of Christ. It indicates the Church's call to nurture, teach, and protect believers in Jesus Christ. In the Second Letter of John, the apostle uses a similar feminine reference for the Church community (see verse 1).

Getting Started

The Second Letter of John is the shortest book of the Bible. It contains only thirteen verses in one chapter. It's an easy read in one sitting.

Concluding Prayer

Lord Jesus,
you are true God and true man;
give us life in you.
Show us the way.
Protect us from the deceiver.
Guard us against antichrists.
Give us eyes to see,
ears to hear,
and hearts to trust your revelation.
Keep us close to you.

We believe in you. We love you.
Show us your glory.
For you are Lord forever and ever.
Amen.

Third John

I have written something to the Church; but Diotrephes, who likes to put himself first, does not acknowledge my authority.

3 JOHN 9

Opening Prayer

Lord Jesus,
you are the source of all that is good;
we thank you and praise you!
Help us to live your way.
Grant us your grace to remain faithful.
Keep all confusion away from us.
Enlighten our minds.
Strengthen our hearts.
Grant us your salvation.
For you are Lord forever and ever.
Amen.

Basic Message

We must remain faithful to the Lord Jesus, do what is good, avoid what is evil, and provide hospitality to those in need.

Introductory Overview

In the Third Letter of John, the apostle addresses Gaius, most likely a good friend of Saint John, who held some local prominence and was well known for his hospitality. The letter praises Gaius for his kindness and criticizes a certain Diotrephes for his

disobedience and arrogance. Saint John encourages Gaius to remain steadfast in his faith and continue in his kindness.

Third John contains only one chapter, so citations from
Third John include only the verses. For example, "3 John 9"
means Third John, chapter 1, verse 9.

Basic Outline
The Third Letter of John consists of five main parts within a
single chapter:

- Verses 1–4: Introduction.
- Verses 5–8: Praise for Gaius's hospitality.
- Verses 9–10: Criticism for Diotrephes's arrogance.
- Verses 11–12: Praise for Demetrius.
- Verses 13–15: Conclusion.

Application to Our Lives
In the Third Letter of John, the apostle emphasizes the importance of hospitality. He praises Gaius's faith and his kindness to
others, even to those whom he doesn't know. The apostle's praise,
however, changes as he writes of a certain Diotrephes. In verses 9–10, John says Diotrephes puts himself first and disregards
John's apostolic authority. Diotrephes also does not welcome
others and expels those who attempt to do so. He is a man of
recognized pride and arrogance. John writes that if he is able to
visit the community, he will call out Diotrephes.

In our lives, we have to be careful of the spirit of Diotrephes.
Pride is a sly and boastful spirit. It cannot accept direction or
correction. A heart enslaved to pride seeks to impose itself on
others. Saint John reminds us that humility and gratitude, kindness and hospitality are the best spiritual weapons against such
a wicked spirit. Abandon pride. Follow the path of humility and
kindness.

Basic Points

Author: The Christian tradition attributes the Third Letter of John to the apostle John, brother of James and son of Zebedee.

Placement: Third John is the twenty-fifth book of the New Testament and the seventy-first book of the Bible. It is the third of three letters written by Saint John.

Keywords:

- Hospitality: A spirit of selfless service that is marked by warmth, welcome, and a deep sense of caring for others, which includes both their material and spiritual well-being. Christians are called to be a people of hospitality.

Getting Started

The Third Letter of John contains only fifteen verses in one chapter. It's an easy read in one sitting.

Concluding Prayer

Lord Jesus,
you give us your divine hospitality.
You call us to humility and gratitude.
Dispel pride from our hearts.
Show us your way.
Help us to welcome others.
Grant us your salvation.
For you are Lord forever and ever.
Amen.

Jude

*These are grumblers, malcontents, following
their own passions, loud-mouthed boasters,
flattering people to gain advantage.*

JUDE 16

Opening Prayer

Lord Jesus,
eternal God and our only Savior,
come to us and guide us.
Help us to remain faithful to you.
Remove false teachers.
Strengthen our hearts.
You are our only hope.
Grant us your salvation.
For you are Lord forever and ever.
Amen.

Basic Message

We must remain faithful to the teachings and way of the Lord
Jesus. We must avoid false teachers.

Introductory Overview

In the Letter of Jude, the author identifies himself as a brother
of James. He is also, therefore, a kinsman of the Lord Jesus. He
addresses diverse communities of mainly Gentile Christians.
He calls them to remain faithful to the Lord and thus the teach-

ings the apostles have given them. He also warns against false teachers.

Jude contains only one chapter, so citations from Jude include only the verses. For example, "Jude 16" means Jude, chapter 1, verse 16.

Basic Outline

The Book of Jude consists of four main parts within a single chapter:

- Verses 1–4: Introduction.
- Verses 5–16: A warning and judgment against false teachers.
- Verses 17–23: The call to live by the apostolic Faith.
- Verses 24–25: Conclusion.

Application to Our Lives

In Jude 5–16, the apostle warns against false teachers. He describes them in a warning to believers, so they can identify false teachers and not imitate their ways. In particular, the apostle denounces the grumbling, bombastic speech, and flattery of false teachers. He also points us to the power of the spoken word, letting us know that certain speech indicates that one is far from the way of the Lord.

In our lives, we must guard our tongues. We praise God with our speech, and so we should use our voices to speak truth, build others up, and promote goodness and beauty. Our ability to speak, to use our tongues, is a gift from God. We need to exercise discipline and prudence in what we say and how we say it. We need to be attentive and avoid all grumbling, angered speech, and flattery and instead speak words of encouragement, gentleness, and truthfulness.

Basic Points

Author: The Christian tradition attributes the Letter of Jude to Jude, brother of James and kinsman of the Lord Jesus.

Placement: Jude is the twenty-sixth book of the New Testament and the seventy-second book of the Bible.

Keywords:

- Flattery: An exaggeration of truth that's used to win the favor or recognition of another. It is a deceptive use of speech that indicates a lack of integrity.

Getting Started

The Letter of Jude contains only twenty-five verses in one chapter. It's an easy read in one sitting.

Concluding Prayer

Lord Jesus,
God and Savior,
we turn to you and seek your grace.
Spare us from the fallenness of our world.
Give us your grace and truth.
Strengthen our hearts.
Help us to persevere.
Grant us your salvation.
For you are Lord forever and ever.
Amen.

Apocalyptic Book

Revelation*

Revelation

When I saw him, I fell at his feet as though dead.
But he laid his right hand upon me, saying,
"Fear not, I am the first and the last."

Opening Prayer

Lord Jesus,
the Alpha and Omega, the Beginning and End of all things,
you come to us and bless us.
We love you. We praise you.
Heal the wounds of our sin.
Restore us to your grace.
Grant us your salvation.
For you are Lord forever and ever.
Amen.

Basic Message

God is all-holy and the Victor over all things. The Lord Jesus has
defeated the power of the Evil One. If we remain faithful to Jesus, despite our sufferings and persecution, we will triumph and
dwell with him forever in heaven.

Introductory Overview

In the Book of Revelation, Saint John recounts his various mystical experiences in a highly symbolic, apocalyptic style. He shows
us that all things are fulfilled in Jesus Christ, who is God and

318

Savior, Lord and Victor. John wrote Revelation at a time when the Roman Empire intensely persecuted the Church, so his message would have given the early Christians much-needed encouragement and inspiration to persevere in their faith.

Basic Outline
The Book of Revelation has seven main parts:

- Chapter 1:1–3: Introduction.
- Chapters 1:4—3: Letters to the seven churches of Asia.
- Chapters 4–5: God and the Lamb.
- Chapters 6–16: The various sequences of seven.
- Chapters 17–20: God's punishment on the unbelieving nations.
- Chapters 21—22:5: A new creation in Jesus Christ.
- Chapter 22:6–21: Conclusion.

Application to Our Lives
In Revelation 1, Saint John describes seeing the Lord Jesus. Once he recognizes him, he falls on his face. He is completely overwhelmed by the glorious presence of the Lord. He tells us that he fell and was like a dead man. The Lord, always merciful and kind, approaches him and places his hand on him, saying, "Fear not." There is nothing to fear. The Lord is Judge, but he is also Savior, and nothing has power over him.

In our lives, there can be things that overwhelm us, break our hearts, shatter our spirits, fill us with fright, confuse us to bewilderment, and shock us into disbelief. In those moments, and in the situations that caused them, we can know the Lord's presence, feel his hand on our heads, receive the strength we need, and hear him say to us, "Fear not." The Lord is with us. He lifts us up, heals us, consoles us, accompanies us through the darkness of this world, and welcomes us into heaven. He is Victor. *Nothing* has power over him, because he is our invincible Savior, who will never abandon us.

Basic Points

Author: The Christian tradition attributes the Book of Revelation to the apostle John, brother of James and son of Zebedee.

Placement: Revelation is the twenty-seventh book of the New Testament and the seventy-third and last book of the Bible. Revelation is the fifteenth of the principal narrative books of the Bible. (See Appendix A.)

Keywords:

- Apocalypse: An unveiling or revelation. Culturally, at the time of the apostles, it was the removal of the veil of a bride before her husband. The imagery reflects the message of the Book of Revelation, which is also known as the Book of the Apocalypse, as it depicts the glory of the Church being revealed to, through, and in Jesus Christ.
- Apocalyptic literature: A mystical writing style that merges time and space in order to give supernatural lessons that transcend human reason. It was an ancient writing style among God's people. Saint John uses this literary style to express his mystical visions, which no human words could fully explain.

Getting Started

While the eventual goal is to read all twenty-one chapters of the Book of Revelation, here are four selections that can help get us started: the coming of Christ (1:7–8); the Lamb standing and slaughtered (5:6–14); the demise of Satan at the end of time (20:11–14); and the new heavens and the new earth (21:1–8).

Concluding Prayer

Lord Jesus,
Lion of the tribe of Judah,
Root of David,
show us your glory!
Unveil your majesty!
Show us your splendor!
We adore you!
We fall to our knees and hail you alone.
We worship you,
O living Lamb of God.
Save us! Redeem us!
Show us your glory!
For you are Lord forever and ever.
Amen.

Conclusion

Therefore take the whole armor of God, that you may be able to withstand in the evil day, and having done all, to stand. ... And take the helmet of salvation, and the sword of the Spirit, which is the word of God.

EPHESIANS 6:13, 17

Our walk through the seventy-three books of the Bible has come to a close. Some books have probably stood out for you, others perhaps not (at least for now). By making this spiritual journey, however, you have allowed yourself to encounter the living word of God. Following the counsel of Saint Paul, you have taken up the whole armor of God and allowed your heart to be fortified, enriched, and convicted in the ways of God.

"Did not our hearts burn within us ..."

As you walked through the Bible, perhaps you felt the same experience of the disciples on the way to Emmaus. As the two were walking together, the Lord Jesus approached them. The conversation continued, and the Lord began to give biblical instruction on the Anointed Savior. Later, as the two disciples recalled the instruction, they were elated and exclaimed, "Did not our hearts burn within us while he talked to us on the road, while he opened to us the Scriptures?" (Lk 24:32).

Yes, our hearts can also burn within us as we encounter the Lord Jesus and allow Sacred Scripture to teach us. We just have to pick up the Bible and read!

Where Do We Go from Here?

After a brief respite, it's good to jump back into the Bible.

Our world is busy, and our lives have many twists and turns, and so it's easy to see the completion of this book as a victory, get distracted, and let the Bible fade away from our lives. We have to avoid this temptation. We need to come up with a plan and stay focused and let the living word of God be a part of our lives.

As Saint Paul reminds us:

Let the word of Christ dwell in you richly, as you teach and admonish one another in all wisdom, and as you sing psalms and hymns and spiritual songs with thankfulness in your hearts to God. (Colossians 3:16)

For whatever was written in former days was written for our instruction, that by steadfastness and by the encouragement of the Scriptures we might have hope. (Romans 15:4)

With this encouragement in mind, here are some general suggestions:

- Read through the Book of Proverbs in the Old Testament every day. There are 31 proverbs, and there are 31 days in a full month. You can read the "proverb of the day" by matching the day of the month with the proverb of the same number.
- Read 5 psalms from the Book of Psalms in the Old Testament every day for a month. There are 150 psalms. If you read 5 a day, you can finish in 30 days. You could read 2 psalms in the morning, 1 at lunch, and 2 in the evening.
- Select one of the prophets from the Old Testament

and focus on the teachings of that book. Many of the prophetic teachings are still very applicable to our world today.

- Read the Gospel of Mark. It's the shortest Gospel Book of the New Testament, with only 16 relatively short chapters. If you read a chapter a day, you can finish the Gospel in a little over 2 weeks.
- Read the Gospel of Luke in the New Testament. It has 24 chapters. You can read a chapter a day and finish the Gospel in under a month. This is a great idea in general, but especially for the month of December. Starting the Gospel of Luke on December 1 will lead you right into Christmas Eve.
- Read through all the Gospel Books of the New Testament in the course of a liturgical season (such as Advent or Lent) or a calendar season (such as the summer).
- Read one of the universal letters of the New Testament. They are less dense than Saint Paul's letters and can make a good introduction to all the letters of the New Testament. Some of these letters can be read in one sitting. Remember, the Second Letter of John has only 13 verses in a single chapter!
- Read all of the narrative books of the Bible.
- Read the specific books of a specific time period in salvation history.
- Read the entire Bible in a year, perhaps using this book as a resource.

There are even more ways of reading the Bible, but these few suggestions will help get you started. The most important thing — through whichever idea or program you follow — is that you continue to read, study, pray, and live the word of God!

"The Lord bless you ..."

As we conclude this walk through the books of the Bible, may you always know God's love and mercy. May you always find in the written word of God the wisdom, instruction, and inspiration you need throughout the journey of life.

May you draw close to the living God through the Bible, and may you always find it to be a lamp to your feet and a bright light to your heart.

As Aaron prayed over the people of God, so this prayer is offered over you:

> The LORD bless you and keep you:
> the LORD make his face to shine upon you,
>   and be gracious to you:
> the LORD lift up his countenance upon you,
>   and give you peace.
> (Numbers 6:24–26)

Appendix A
The Narrative Books

Although the Bible consists of seventy-three distinct books, the base storyline of salvation is contained within a smaller group of narrative books. Oftentimes, when people say they want to read "the whole Bible," they usually mean that they want to know the story of salvation.

While it's good to read all seventy-three books of the Bible, it might be better for new Bible readers to read the narrative books first.

The list of narrative books, however, is not set in stone. Scholars disagree over which books should be listed as narrative books. With that said, the generally accepted list of narrative books comprises these fifteen books of the Bible:

- Genesis: Early, prehistory salvation history and the era of the patriarchs
- Exodus: The enslavement of God's people in Egypt and their liberation
- Numbers: The time of the purification of God's people in the desert
- Joshua: The conquest of the Promised Land
- Judges: The settlement period of the Promised Land
- First Samuel: The establishment of David's throne
- Second Samuel: The rule of David as king of Israel
- First Kings: The rule of Solomon, the dedication of the Temple, and the division of David's kingdom
- Second Kings: The invasion of the Assyrians and the Babylonians; the fall of Jerusalem and the de-

struction of the Temple
- Ezra: The building of the Second Temple
- Nehemiah: The rebuilding of Jerusalem
- First Maccabees: The Greek occupation
- Gospel of Luke: The life and teachings of Jesus Christ, the Anointed Savior
- Acts of the Apostles: The witness of the early Church
- Revelation: The fulfillment of all things in Jesus Christ

Appendix B
The Deuterocanonical Books

The deuterocanonical books are the seven books found in the Catholic Bible that are not contained in the Protestant Bible.

The term *deuterocanonical* means "second list." The name indicates the history of these books and explains why there is a discrepancy within two Christian traditions.

The Old Testament was originally written in Hebrew. As God's people entered the time of the Second Temple with the eventual Greek occupation, the question was asked whether the Old Testament could be translated into Greek. It was a serious theological question, since the Old Testament had never been translated or preserved in a language other than Hebrew.

Jewish leaders decided that the Old Testament could be translated into Greek, so that God's wisdom could be better known by his people and other people of goodwill.

When the Old Testament was translated into Greek (what is called the Septuagint), seven other books that were revered by God's people were included in the translation. This was the "second list," since it included additional books.

The larger canon of books was broadly accepted and used by God's people for study and prayer. So the additional books helped mold and shape the faith and worship of God's people during the period of the Second Temple. It is highly probable that the Lord Jesus, as a member of God's people during the time of the Second Temple, read, studied, proclaimed, and was shaped in his human nature by the teachings contained in the deuterocanonical books.

In addition, the deuterocanonical books were part of the entire Christian way of life until the time of the Protestant Reformation. At that time, the Reformers removed the deuterocanonical books from the Bible and went back to the pre-Septuagint list of books. The deuterocanonical books are sometimes called the "apocrypha" in the Protestant tradition.

The deuterocanonical books are:

- Tobit (historical book)
- Judith (historical book)
- First Maccabees (historical book)
- Second Maccabees (historical book)
- Wisdom (wisdom book)
- Sirach (wisdom book)
- Baruch (prophetic book)

Bibliography

General Sources

The Ignatius Bible: *Revised Standard Version — Second Catholic Edition*. San Francisco: Ignatius Press, 2005.

Other Sources

Baker, Kenneth. *Inside the Bible*. San Francisco: Ignatius Press, 1998.

Bergsma, John. *Bible Basics for Catholics*. Notre Dame, IN: Ave Maria Press, 2012.

Gray, Tim, and Jeff Cavins. *Walking with God*. West Chester, PA: Ascension Press, 2010.

Hahn, Scott. *A Father Who Keeps His Promises*. Ann Arbor, MI: Servant Publications, 1998.

Kreeft, Peter. *You Can Understand the Bible*. San Francisco: Ignatius Press, 2005.

Laux, John. *Introduction to the Bible*. Charlotte, NC: TAN Books, 1990.

Martin, George. *Scripture Footnotes*. Huntington, IN: Our Sunday Visitor Publishing, 2017.

Schehr, Timothy. *The Bible Made Easy*. Cincinnati, OH: St. Anthony Messenger Press, 2006.

Shea, Mark. *Making Senses Out of Scripture*. Dallas: Basilica Press, 1999.

Sri, Edward. *The Bible Compass*. West Chester, PA: Ascension Press, 2009.

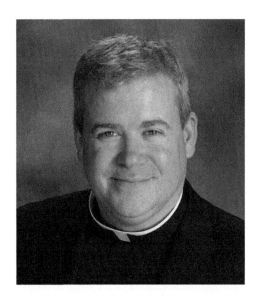

About the Author

Fr. Jeffrey Kirby, STD, is a moral theologian and the pastor of Our Lady of Grace Parish in Indian Land, South Carolina. He is an adjunct professor of theology at Belmont Abbey College, where he teaches introductory courses in the Bible. Fr. Kirby is the author of several books, including *Living in Peace* and *Way of the Cross for Loved Ones Who Have Left the Faith.*